LIBRARY TRAINING GUIDES

Series Editor: David Baker
Editorial Assistant: Joan Welsby

CLHBEC

Introduction by the Series Editor

This new series of Library Training Guides (LTGs for short) aims to fill the gap left by the demise of the old Training Guidelines published in the 1980s in the wake of the Library Association's work on staff training. The new LTGs develop the original concept of concisely written summaries of the best principles and practice in specific areas of training by experts in the field which give library and information workers a good-quality guide to best practice. Like the original guidelines, the LTGs also include appropriate examples from a variety of library systems as well as further reading and useful contacts.

Though each guide stands in its own right, LTGs form a coherent whole. Acquisition of all LTGs as they are published will result in a comprehensive manual of training and staff development in library and information work.

The guides are aimed at practising librarians and library training officers. They are intended to be comprehensive without being over-detailed; they should give both the novice and the experienced librarian/training officer an overview of what should/could be done in a given situation and in relation to a particular skill/group of library staff/type of library.

David Baker

LIBRARY TRAINING GUIDES

Interpersonal skills

Philippa Levy

Library Association Publishing

© Library Association Publishing Ltd 1993

Published by
Library Association Publishing Ltd
7 Ridgmount Street
London WC1E 7AE

First published 1993

British Library Cataloguing in Publication Data. A catalogue record for this book is available from the British Library.

ISBN 1-85604-081-X

Typeset in 11/12pt Palermo from author's disk by Library Association Publishing Ltd
Printed and made in Great Britain by Amber (Printwork) Ltd, Harpenden, Herts.

Contents

1 Introduction

1.1 The Guide

This Guide aims to provide a concise and practical overview of key issues relating to in-house design and delivery of interpersonal skills training (IST) for library staff. IST in this context is defined as off-the-job training input which is designed to enhance participants' personal awareness, confidence and competence in interacting with others at work, whether clients or colleagues. The Guide focuses on workshop-based IST because of the importance of participative group-work in interpersonal skills development. However, this type of training provision can be combined productively with other formats; for instance, well-designed distance- or open-learning materials aimed at individual learners can offer useful support for participative learning, and on-the-job coaching has an important contribution to make to ongoing skills development.

IST is relevant to all levels of library staff and covers a multitude of topics, so the focus of the Guide is on general principles rather than on particular IST topics. As a means of showing how principles can be applied in practice, the discussion is supported by examples of overall workshop design and some detailed descriptions of particular activities.

It is hoped that library training officers and others with training and staff development involvement will find the Guide's approach useful – whether for organizing a customer care or induction programme for front-line staff, a management development event, or any other training activity relating to the 'people' side of library work. It is unlikely that all of a library's IST needs will be fulfilled by in-house training staff, since specialist or outside input will be more appropriate for some topics, and the use of external trainers (from the library's parent institution, professional associations, or other training providers) certainly need not be prohibitively expensive.

On the other hand, the development of effective IST strategy depends on the existence of in-house expertise, and it is probable that for most medium-sized and large library services at least, the ability of library staff to provide responsive, flexible and cost-effective IST will be crucial to that strategy. For those library trainers with little or no prior experience of planning or leading IST events, the Guide is intended as an introductory source of ideas; for others, perhaps it will offer some new perspectives. Within the general framework of participative, experiential IST, there is plenty of scope for individual creativity in designing and delivering events which will be closely tailored to the particular needs and interests of each training group.

The Guide is divided into six main chapters. The first is introductory and covers issues relating to the rationale for IST provision in libraries, and the range of skills in question. The following chapters look in turn at the five basic stages of the IST cycle, highlighting major considerations involved at each one:

- Assessment of IST needs
- Establishment of training aims and objectives
- Design and preparation of IST event
- Delivery of IST event
- Post-training evaluation

A concluding chapter summarizes main IST planning points in the form of a brief checklist, and appendices include a resource list and a selection of sample 'real-life' IST workshop outlines and materials from a variety of libraries.

1.2 The aims of IST

Organization development

It is increasingly recognized that high-quality, user-centred library service depends in great part on the strength of the 'people' orientation of the organization, and that this means paying attention not only to the quality of front-line interactions between staff and users, but to the interpersonal health of the organization as a whole. Given the inevitable and all-important knock-on effect which exists between an organization's internal interpersonal culture and its external relations, the promotion and maintenance of effective management style and colleague relations is crucial for building user-oriented library service. Where individual staff training needs at all levels are recognized and addressed as part of an holistic organizational development strategy, IST can contribute much to the planned evolution of people-oriented libraries. Inevitably, difficulties are presented by resourcing constraints, and IST has to compete with technical training for resource allocation. However, although IST may be viewed as a lower priority, especially in the wake of technological advances, the need for technical training should not conceal the existence of needs for IST which may be equally pressing.

Staff development

Participants in IST sometimes express doubts about whether it is actually possible to improve interpersonal skills by means of training. Scepticism can arise when success in interpersonal relationships is viewed as a matter of innate personal qualities which individuals either possess or lack; consequently, interpersonal problems are taken to be the result of unavoidable 'personality clashes'. From this point of view it can often seem that many interpersonal difficulties in organizations are too big or too deep-rooted to be amenable to change. Another view is that while interpersonal behaviour might not be inherent, skills are best learned in the natural course of events 'on the job', and that training away from the workplace will be artificial and ineffective. Still others may be suspicious of the aims of IST, feeling that such training should be approached with caution because it may set out to change the essence of individual personalities by imposing new behaviours in a mechanistic fashion. In contrast to these perspectives, this Guide takes the positive position that while IST is by no means a panacea, when carefully designed and facilitated it has the potential to provide meaningful and productive opportunities for personal development which can feed into organizational effectiveness.

Far from being innate, much human behaviour is learned, and all people exhibit both strengths and weaknesses in their habitual ways of dealing with interpersonal situations. Listening ability is one case in point; a person may be good at paying close attention and understanding what another person is saying, but not so skilled in communicating this understanding. A useful definition of interpersonal competence is that it is the ability to make an appropriate sequence of choices about behaviour and to put these into practice in order to achieve a desired goal.[1] In order for this to be accomplished, an appropriate combination of knowledge, attitudes and skill has to be brought to bear on the situation. For instance, to communicate effectively with student library users from another country, academic library staff might need to be aware of the expectations that the students are likely to have of the library, to adopt an open-minded attitude to a different behavioural style, and to be skilled in interpreting non-verbal as well as verbal messages. They should also need to be aware of any of their own attitudes or behaviours which could act as barriers to successful communication.

The overall aim of IST is therefore to provide participants with a framework for learning at the levels of knowledge, attitude and skills, and to encourage the transfer of learning from the training event to the work environment.[2] Effective IST enables participants to evaluate their own strengths and weaknesses and to make informed decisions about areas in which they could do things differently, or about skills on which they could build. To achieve this, workshop opportunities are provided to develop personal awareness, to identify an appropriate range of behavioural choices for any given situation, and to try out or assess the various options. From this process, it becomes possible to make decisions about changes to behaviour in interactions at work.[3]

Analysed from a skills perspective, 'personality clashes' and apparently unsolvable communication problems at work can very often be understood in terms of ineffective behavioural choices. In other words, viewed in these terms, IST is not about trying to change personalities, but about providing opportunities for people to come to their own decisions about what may be relevant to them and their work roles. These aims can be pointed out to participants, along with the point that any IST event can only be part of a continuous process of development, hopefully providing impetus for further skills development in 'real life'. Acceptance of IST can be very much a question of how it is marketed to staff, both during training and more generally: it needs to be promoted positively within the library as a means of building on both personal and organizational strengths, rather than as a strategy for imposing remedial treatment.

Training and therapy

Participants in IST understandably may be anxious or confused about the grey area that seems to exist between some forms of training and therapy. It may be worth making it clear at the outset of an IST event that what is being offered is training, not therapy. IST approaches which focus strongly on participants' feelings can come close to therapy, and there are some parallels between the skills of the trainer and the counsellor or therapist. However, although some of the issues touched on in IST may be deep ones, there are important distinctions between the two processes. A major one is that therapy often focuses in a sustained way on the past as a way of understanding present behaviours and feelings, and may actively encourage cathartic release. IST aims to offer opportunities to increase personal effectiveness in relationships, but does not attempt to address issues in the same depth as therapy. On the other hand, participants in IST may sometimes choose to deal with difficult personal issues, or find that uncomfortable feelings are triggered by the training, and trainers need to be able to respond sensitively and effectively if this happens.

1.3 Defining interpersonal skills

In setting out to explore and identify skilled behaviour with groups of people, there can be a danger of imposing concepts of skill which are ethnocentric or limited in other ways. If IST is to be meaningful and therefore successful, it is important to take cultural and other contextual considerations into account and to acknowledge that the value placed on different behaviours tends to be determined by factors such as culture, social class, gender and race. These factors shape behaviour and underpin definitions of what is acceptable, desirable and skilled; behaviour that is appropriate in one context may be disastrous in another, and what is accepted as skilled in one person's view or in one setting may appear quite unskilled to someone else or in another environment. For instance, cultural and gender considerations influence how and how much people engage in self-disclosure (revealing personal information) at work.

Organizations themselves can be seen as distinct cultures with their own belief-systems and behavioural norms and standards, and this will affect the way in which skills are perceived and defined by staff. Recent research into the interpersonal skills requirements of library and other organizations revealed that while training managers tended to refer to broad skills areas in the same general terms, what they actually meant varied according to organizational ethos and different perspectives on appropriate organizational relationships, roles and management styles.[4] It is important that the approach to IST adopted by an organization should 'fit' with its culture or with its strategy of culture change.

Of course, it may be that very different perspectives on the nature of interpersonal skill are held by staff in the same organization. It cannot be assumed that participants in IST groups will all hold the same views on the way in which skilled behaviour should be defined, and perhaps participants will wish to contest the assumptions held by others or taken for granted and promoted at an organizational level. For example, concepts of effective management style and skills can be very variable, as can cultural judgements about the value of assertiveness or the nature of appropriate listening behaviour. For some cultural groups, eye contact is a powerful signal of listening, whereas for others, avoidance of eye contact is associated with the expression of respect and does not mean that listening is not occurring. Trainers should beware of recommending such skills in terms of universal formulae. Since skilled communication is based on awareness of self and of contextual values and norms, IST should offer participants the opportunity to reach definitions of skill by exploring different viewpoints within the group and by reflecting critically on their own perspectives, as well as through experimentation with new techniques or ideas.

A range of communication models is available to support IST, each having particular strengths and likely to be used in accordance with specific training objectives and the background of the trainer. Models such as Transactional Analysis, Egan's 'Helping Skills' framework and Heron's 'Six-category Intervention Analysis' may also be found valuable in library IST.[5,6,7]

1.4 Interpersonal skills for library work

Figure 1 (p.59) shows in general terms the interpersonal skills required for UK library work, as identified by the research mentioned above and originally presented in the research report. The model – which could no doubt be added to – is a powerful illustration of the variety and complexity of the interpersonal dimension of library work. Skills areas are grouped according to four spheres of activity in library work – self-management, managing and supervising others, teamwork and client interactions – in accordance with the main concerns of the public and academic librarians surveyed. Since there are overlaps in the types of interaction and skills involved in these work spheres, it could be argued persuasively that some skills could be placed in a different quadrant, or in more than one. Moreover, as argued above, it is not possible to define interpersonal skills satisfactorily out of context, and some of the skills described below will not be applicable to all circumstances. The arrangement is therefore proposed simply as a general working framework, which may be of help as a starting-point for identifying local organizational requirements and for planning training initiatives.

In general, it is likely that staff will need to handle increasingly complex situations as they rise in the organization or take on new responsibilities. For instance, training in basic counselling techniques, which are helpful in supporting other people to think through and manage their own problems effectively, might become important when a member of staff moves into a middle-management role such as head of department or branch manager. New IST needs for staff also emerge at times of organizational change. Changes in staffing structures may lead to a focus on developing team-building and teamwork skills, or increased pressures on the service may give rise to a need to explore particular client relations problems. Whether staff wish to 'brush up' on skills that have been part of their work for a long time, or move towards developing new areas of skill, individual participation in IST should be planned logically, so that the direction of personal development fits in closely with work demands.

Core skills
The model identifies a number of core communication skills which function as the foundation for effective interactions of many kinds, whether between colleagues or between staff and library users. Becoming more aware of the relevance of core skills to many different types of interpersonal situation at work encourages a 'rounded' approach to personal development and fosters individual flexibility rather than mechanistic application of techniques. It is important to approach skills development in a logical learning sequence. Some core skills provide a foundation for others; for instance, it makes sense to consolidate understanding of the purposes and techniques of active listening before tackling challenging skills or skills in giving critical feedback. Equally, a firm grounding in core skills is a productive point of departure for focusing more closely on the specifics of particular types of interaction. In order to conduct an appraisal interview effectively, for example, a manager needs to know how to use active listening and feedback skills and why they are relevant to appraisal, as well as to understand the particular demands and procedures of the appraisal process.

A recent IST course attended by university library staff was designed with these principles in mind.[8] Based on feedback from staff about their training interests and needs, the programme first offered six two-hour core skills workshop sessions, exploring the relevance of the skills to a variety of common interpersonal scenarios in library work. The sessions covered aspects of verbal and non-verbal communication, active listening, feedback and assertiveness and were followed by four further workshops, each of which looked in more depth at the specific requirements of one type of interpersonal involvement, such as working with international users and reference work.

Some of the core skills are outlined below. They, and all the other skills identified on the model, are described in more detail in the texts included in the resource list (Appendix 1).

Active listening   First and foremost, perhaps, the skills associated with active listening deserve to be highlighted. Good listening is the basis of most effective communication, although it can only too easily be taken for granted or, conversely, forgotten at moments of difficulty. However, being able to pay really good attention to another person's non-verbal and verbal messages, and to reach an accurate understanding of his or her perspective, depends on a combination of awareness, open-mindedness and skill which is not always easily achieved. Active listening entails both receptivity and communication ability, and is of use in situations in which the listener's goal is to encourage participation, seek feedback, ensure consultation or perhaps take a counselling approach to problem-solving. It applies to working with clients, as in reference interviewing and dealing with informal enquiries, as well as to many types of formal and informal interactions between staff, and can be seen as an enabling or motivational tool, as well as having a place in conflict management. The skills involved include the ability to exercise empathy (to understand an issue or problem from someone else's viewpoint), to paraphrase, summarize and use open questions, and to adopt appropriate body language.

Contextual and self-awareness   As has already been indicated, understanding of the nature and impact of one's own behaviour, and of the factors which shape it and the behaviour of others, is vital if barriers to effective communication are to be recognized and transcended. Attempts to exercise empathy are bound to be impeded by the fact that people perceive behaviour differently, whether due to cultural, social or other more personal factors. Many forms of contextual communication barrier may operate between colleagues or between staff and clients in libraries, with negative consequences, not least in relation to equal opportunities issues. Awareness of issues relating to gender, sexuality, race, physical ability, class and concepts of management style is crucial in feeding into effective and appropriate interpersonal behaviour, and awareness-raising of this kind is an important component of library IST.

Library IST events can be dedicated to the topic of cross-cultural communication with users, perhaps in relation to international groups, or to groups such as the elderly, teenagers, the unemployed, people living within the mental health system, part-time students and others – and to the impact that their circumstances and needs might have on the quality and nature of interactions between them and library staff. Less obvious, perhaps, are contextual barriers which may operate between colleagues; it is worth noting, for instance, that communication between the sexes can itself be seen as a form of cross-cultural communication.[9]

Giving feedback If libraries are to manage change and staff development effectively, staff at all levels need to be skilled in giving both positive (motivational) feedback and critical (developmental) feedback to colleagues. While positive feedback essentially consists of expressing appreciation where it is due, critical feedback involves giving information which may be less welcome; for instance, about an aspect of work which needs to be improved, or about a perceived problem with behaviour or attitude. Feedback skills are clearly of use in the context of formal staff appraisal sessions, but are also relevant to many informal occasions at work, whether communicating sideways, upwards or downwards in the organizational hierarchy. However, giving feedback effectively is a difficult skill to acquire and consequently can be neglected.

Assertiveness There appears to be a strong consensus among UK library trainers and managers about the value of assertiveness for many aspects of library work. Assertiveness is the expression of direct and honest communication between two individuals in a manner which is respectful of both parties. Often this is put in terms of standing up for one's own rights while recognizing and not violating the rights of the other person. Assertiveness can be contrasted with passive, aggressive and covertly aggressive behaviours, and assertiveness training aims to raise participants' awareness of patterns of behaviour they might habitually adopt and to offer alternative choices. Assertiveness training is strongly associated with personal development for women, but it is equally appropriate to men, and is useful for many organizational circumstances; for instance, for handling conflict, giving feedback, refusing unreasonable demands and negotiating terms or change.

The aim to boost participants' self-confidence is an important part of assertiveness training, but it also offers a set of tried and tested behavioural techniques which, if used successfully, will contribute to developing the person's self-confidence and self-esteem. Some examples of assertive verbal and non-verbal behaviours are: firm tone of voice and reasonably loud speech, direct eye contact, erect posture, absence of negative or distracting habits of body language. Skills in active listening, self-disclosure and open-ended questioning are also associated with assertiveness.[10]

References

1 Nelson-Jones, R., *Human relationship skills*, (2nd edn), London, Cassell, 1991.
2 Dainow, S. and Bailey, C., *Developing skills with people: training for person to person contact*, Chichester, Wiley, 1988.
3 Phillips, K. and Fraser, T., *The management of interpersonal skills training*, Aldershot, Gower, 1982.
4 Levy, P. and Usherwood, B., *People skills: interpersonal skills training for library and information work*, (Library and Information Research Report 88), London, British Library, 1992.
5 Barker, D. M., *TA and training: the theory and use of transactional analysis in organizations*, Aldershot, Gower, 1980.
6 Egan, G., *The skilled helper: a systematic approach to effective helping*, (4th edn), Monterey, California, Brooks/Cole, 1990.
7 Heron, J., *Six category intervention analysis*, (2nd edn), Guildford, Human Potential Resource Group, University of Surrey, 1989.
8 'People Skills in Action' course for staff of Sheffield University Library.

9   Tannen, D., *You just don't understand! Women and men in conversation*, London, Virago, 1991.

10 Kelley, C., *Assertion training: a facilitator's guide*, San Diego, California, University Associates, 1979.

 **Assessment of IST needs**

Planning for IST provision should be based on clear strategic objectives and on responsiveness to members of staff as individuals – which means gaining an understanding of the interpersonal skills development needs of the library as a whole, of its different occupational groups, and of individual members of staff. While one or two special considerations need to be taken into account when conducting training needs analysis (TNA) for IST, in the main general principles apply; a more detailed examination of what is involved in TNA for libraries is provided by the Library Training Guide on this topic.[1]

2.1 Organization-wide and occupational IST needs assessment

There is no doubt that large-scale TNA is time-consuming and resource-intensive, but the pay-off in terms of training effectiveness and the likely promotion of a stronger, shared orientation towards IST within the library is clear. Since IST needs can arise suddenly and may not occur at times of regular reviews, these should be complemented by ongoing investigation of the IST implications of any organizational changes, and should take into account any new IST needs which may emerge in tandem with new occupational or departmental requirements.

The range of methods for collecting information about organizational or occupational skills gaps includes:

- observation of staff behaviour;
- analysis of job specifications;
- staff surveys by questionnaire;
- individual or group interviews and consultation with staff.

Data from client satisfaction surveys may also be used to feed into the process. The frequency with which organization-wide or occupational TNA is carried out, and the methods used, will depend on a variety of factors including resource availability and the nature of the organizational culture. In general, management-led and more 'learner-centred' approaches can be contrasted; current trends in the identification of competences – for instance, national vocational qualifications (NVQs) in the UK – tend to be based on methods which entail systematic management-led task specification and job analysis, whereas in other areas, it is considered important for staff to be made directly responsible for identifying their own, or their occupational group's, training needs. On the whole, it appears that the most useful strategy for IST is a combination of methods involving staff from all parts of the organization in genuine and democratic consultation, contributing to acceptance and shared 'ownership' of the programmes which are developed as a consequence. It is, of course, vital that the feedback process should be two-way, so that contributors to TNA research are able to see where their views and perceptions fit in with or differ from those of their colleagues, and the impact they as individuals have had on the planning process.

In the relatively sensitive area of interpersonal behaviour, the choice of TNA method should take account of people's potential reluctance to communicate their development needs directly to colleagues; thus, the anonymity of questionnaires, despite their limitations for collecting in-depth qualitative data, might in some cases be found more fruitful than face-to-face interviews. In addition, individuals may not be able to specify precisely what their learning needs are in terms of skill, so that often it is more productive to ask for feedback about problems associated with various work activities and situations than about perceived 'core skills' needs. For instance, an individual might identify a problem in interacting with a certain type of user, but not be aware that assertiveness, or active listening skills, could be helpful.

2.2   Assessing personal development needs

In order that IST provision responds to the personal development needs of members of staff, methods of TNA must take into account the accelerating rate of change in library work requirements and experience. Job analyses and skills specifications may become outdated quickly, and so it is important to encourage and build on a proactive, self-directed orientation towards identifying training needs. The more involved staff are in defining their own learning needs, the more meaningful and effective their learning is likely to be. TNA methods at this level generally combine personal involvement with line-management support and feedback (as in formal appraisal procedures, as well as in ongoing discussion and consultation), and techniques which aim to promote self-directed reflection and analysis are becoming increasingly popular. Staff may find self and group perception instruments such as Belbin's Team Roles Questionnaire helpful in this context;[2] other methods include individual action-planning procedures and participation in action-learning sets or focus groups.

The Library Association's Framework for Continuing Education, which aims to promote opportunities for planned personal development, offers a self-directed approach to TNA which could have benefits in the area of interpersonal skills. The Framework invites library staff to analyse the skills requirements of their current and future roles, and from this to identify key development needs and aims. It is recommended that, having identified training needs individually, and drafted a development plan, staff should consult with employers to obtain their views and support and to reach final decisions collaboratively. The procedure could be incorporated into appraisal schemes if these exist, but it also lends itself to less formal circumstances. As is pointed out, collecting copies of individual development plans could be helpful in drawing up training plans on an organization-wide basis.

It is important to plan an individual's participation in IST in a way which avoids the dangers of both over-rigid programming and ad hoc attendance. Staff at the same stage in their career may have quite different IST needs, so any provision linked to major career thresholds (such as supervisory, junior, middle and senior management) should be flexible and responsive to personal circumstances.

Since interpersonal skills acquisition is a gradual, developmental process, it should be treated as such through provision of ongoing and long-term learning opportunities. It would be unrealistic for IST participants or their managers to hope that one-off attendance on a course could ensure sustained behaviour and attitude change, without appropriate follow-up. Courses can be designed with a built-in ongoing feature, for instance, running over a number of weeks or months. Refresher courses may be provided at intervals, or self-development support groups set up to continue the learning process. In addition, on-the-job reinforcement of training is vital, perhaps by providing line-manager or mentor coaching and support for staff as they engage in new or challenging interpersonal responsibilities.

2.3   IST policy: should participation be compulsory?

It is often said that staff who 'most need' IST are the ones who do not attend appropriate training events. This may be because they do not recognize their own needs and have not been helped to do so, or because they are reluctant to become involved in IST for some reason. Given this problem, should attendance on IST events be optional or mandatory? Different libraries will proceed differently here. Clearly, the ideal is for attendance to be voluntary, since for one thing, it is much less likely that useful learning will take place if the participant is resistant to the experience; the challenge to the trainer can be enormous when participants are uncommitted, or confused or resentful about why they have been sent. There is certainly a philosophical contradiction if the training approach emphasizes the principles of individual choice and responsibility in personal development, but participants have not been involved in negotiating their own training decisions and are not attending the event of their own volition.

On the other hand, it may well be considered that the library's strategic commitment to interpersonal skills development is paramount and that participation in some IST is a fundamental requirement of everybody's job. Policy decisions may be clear where corporate programmes for equal opportunities or customer care are concerned, but more difficult to establish in relation to individual participation in other types of IST, and the pros and cons will need to be weighed up according to strategic priorities and management style. On a positive note, however, where a personal development ethos becomes established as part of the organization's culture, and where IST opportunities are sensitively 'marketed' to staff, this may not be too great a problem.

References

1   Williamson, M., *Training needs analysis*, London, Library Association, 1993 (Library Training Guides).

2   Belbin, R.M., *Management teams: why they succeed or fail*, (2nd edn), London, Heinemann, 1989.

3 Establishing training aims and objectives

3.1 What will participants learn?

The next planning step is to set clear aims and objectives for the content of the course. The trainer may do this alone, or in consultation with other staff. Where staff are being encouraged to take more responsibility for their own learning, it is useful – and motivating – for prospective participants in the training to become directly involved in negotiating its aims and objectives, for instance by meeting as a group with the trainer.

3.2 Setting learning aims and objectives

Aims are the overall goals to be achieved by staff as a result of participating in the training; for instance, an IST learning aim might be phrased as follows:

- At the end of training, the managers will be able to identify the skills of giving developmental feedback to staff, and recognize how they could be applied in the context of their work roles.

Another way of putting this would be to phrase it from the trainer's point of view, as follows:

- To enable the managers to identify the skills of giving developmental feedback to staff, and to recognize how they could be applied in the context of their work roles.

Learning objectives are more precise statements of the means by which the general aims are to be achieved. Although the process of clarifying objectives may seem pedantic, without clear objectives it is much more difficult to make appropriate decisions about course design; the objectives also provide the criteria to be used as the basis for evaluation of the event. They should be realistic and measurable, and take the following three factors into account.[1]

- Firstly, they should state in specific terms what the learner could be able to do at the end of training. Since all IST courses will have a cognitive, affective and behavioural dimension, it may be useful to analyse final performance according to desired changes at the levels of knowledge, skills and attitudes. It is important here to use terms which describe behaviour rather than refer to processes like 'knowing', 'understanding' and 'appreciating', which cannot be quantified. Terms like 'identify', 'list' or 'use' are more helpful.
- Secondly, statements of objectives should indicate how participants

will be able to demonstrate their learning; for instance, through solving particular types of problem.

- Thirdly, if possible, the standards which participants should achieve should be stated. Behavioural standards can be difficult to set, and so reference may be made simply to 'the satisfaction of the trainer' or to improvements as assessed by the participants themselves.

Examples of clear learning objectives are the following:

- All participants should be able to identify and list a range of circumstances in which feedback skills could be of use to them in their personal work roles.
- All participants should be able to take the role of appraiser in a staff appraisal role-play, practise the skills associated with giving constructive critical feedback, and assess the level of their own achievement in a potentially difficult interview scenario.

Trainers should guard against setting too many learning objectives for the time available. A useful rule of thumb is that more than two main objectives for a one-day event are likely to be unrealistic. Aims and objectives for a sample course are given at the end of Chapter 4.

3.3 How will participants learn?

In order for learning (or content) aims to be achieved, an appropriate learning environment for interpersonal skills development needs to be established. Several different strands of learning theory have influenced IST practice over recent decades, but probably the most influential at present are the principles of adult and experiential learning which are outlined below. Some background knowledge of these principles is essential for IST trainers, both for planning the design of workshops and for facilitating them successfully; when planning a workshop, it is as important to start with clearly defined process aims as it is to define aims relating to content.

Adult learning

Adult learning theory, or 'androgogy' as it has been called by its foremost theorist and researcher, is based on the following key premises, each of which has important implications for the design of IST events:[2]

- The quality of adult motivation and learning is much enhanced when, instead of being in a position of dependency on the teacher or trainer, participants have the opportunity to be self-directing in all aspects of the learning process. IST participants need to experience 'ownership' of course objectives, content and process, and the trainer therefore has the task of encouraging the capacity for self-motivation and involvement. His or her role is one of facilitator or change agent, ideally involving learners in collaborative planning and identification of training needs and objectives, active contribution to course content and process, and evaluation – and helping to overcome the expectations fostered by traditional education that learners will play a much more passive role.
- Learning which is based on exploration of experience is particularly meaningful and therefore particularly successful. Adults have a good deal of prior experience to draw on, and all participants bring knowl-

edge and insights to the IST group which will provide important learning resources for themselves and for others. Sometimes adult learners believe that they know little or nothing about a topic, but during a participative workshop which invites reflection on and sharing of prior experience, discover that this is not the case at all. In addition to referring to past experience, participants' direct 'here-and-now' experience can be tapped by using the training framework and methods suggested by experiential learning theory.

- Adults become motivated to learn when they perceive a need to do so; for instance, when they believe that what is to be covered during an IST workshop will be of direct relevance and immediately applicable to tasks or problems they face in real life. While key issues should have emerged in the course of the TNA prior to the training event, spending some time focusing on learning needs and interests at the start of the workshop will be of benefit to both trainer and participants. If, as may happen for logistical reasons, participants have not been very involved in TNA or in setting the training objectives, they may arrive with rather generalized aims, or feeling uncertain about what they want to get out of participating. Commitment to engage in the training will be enhanced if they are given a chance to identify personal interests as specifically as possible at the start of the workshop, and throughout there should be ample opportunity for exploration and discussion of personal perspectives. In addition, while the overall structure and content of the course will usually be pre-planned, it can be helpful if the trainer comes prepared with a choice of activities or topics for some parts of it, in order to respond actively and flexibly to participants' concerns.

Experiential learning

Developing interpersonal skills involves cognitive, affective and behavioural change. Each dimension requires a different 'way in' to learning, and so it is important that workshops offer participants a balanced mix of learning activities which together provide the opportunity for making changes in their knowledge, attitudes and skills. Gaining new information on a communication topic, for example by means of a short lecture, may change how they think about it, but this alone is unlikely to affect behaviour or attitudes. Behavioural skills are most effectively developed through practice, and then by experiencing and gaining feedback on the results of that practice. In general, attitudes change slowly and with difficulty, but learning activities which engage participants' feelings – such as experiencing a new situation, perhaps from someone else's point of view – may contribute to helpful shifts in perspective.

Kolb's model of the experiential learning cycle is a widely-used framework, based on extensive research, for designing IST workshops which aim to engage the 'whole person' in learning (see Figure 2, p.60). It shows how learning occurs when we engage fully in an experience (including at a 'feeling' level), are able to look back on it critically, gain some useful insight from it, and go on to make a decision to make a change in our behaviour as a result.[3] Understanding learning as an holistic process has implications for the way in which IST activities should be combined and sequenced. A useful way of approaching IST workshop design is to see the event as a series of structured experiences which enable participants to engage in all aspects of the learning cycle. This means that vital learning ingredients of a balanced IST session will be as follows:

- *Involvement in an experiential activity.* The most significant aspect of Kolb's model is its emphasis on the need to use concrete experience as the point of departure for engaging in reflection and conceptualization. Almost any activity which invites personal involvement (through individual reflection or interpersonal interaction) can be used to provide this experience, such as filling in self-perception instruments, discussing ideas and feelings in a group, watching a trigger video, role-playing or engaging in group-based problem-solving.

  It is important to recognize that these activities are the means of setting the learning process in motion, rather than its end-point. A common mistake in designing IST events is to devote most of the time available to participation in this kind of exercise, leaving insufficient time for group members to engage in the processes represented by the following stages of the learning cycle. If this happens, the learners are unlikely to be able to assimilate and internalize the experience adequately, and may well end up feeling frustrated and disillusioned with the potential of IST to make any real impact.

- *Structured opportunities for personal reflection and for giving and receiving feedback* (information about how an individual's behaviour or views appear to others or otherwise affect them). It is easy to neglect these debriefing stages, especially the opportunity for group members to reflect back systematically on the experience; however, the value of reflection and feedback can hardly be over-emphasized. Visual or sound recordings can be extremely powerful in illuminating the experiential activity retrospectively, but 'lower-tech' alternatives can be equally successful.

  One way of setting up a reflection exercise is to ask group members to form pairs and to take turns in thinking about and answering a few well-defined questions about what happened during the experiential activity (for example, a role-play), and what their reactions (thoughts and feelings) to it are. Feedback can be exchanged directly by participants, on the basis either of observation or of shared involvement in the experience. Structure is important – debriefing discussions can easily become too open-ended or unfocused, so much depends on how they are organized, the quality of instructions given to participants, and the trainer's skills in facilitating group interaction.

- *Identification of general principles.* This is the point at which group members have the opportunity to think about how their analysis of the activity relates more generally to comparable situations at work. They might, for instance, be asked to reflect as individuals, and to write down, what they feel they have learned from it. This is often a useful time for the trainer to provide some theory input, in the form of a brief presentation, in order to reinforce or amplify participants' discussion. Using theory to help draw together and frame conclusions identified by participants, rather than to set the scene in a directive way, is consistent with the aim to encourage inductive learning. A workshop which starts with a long lecture telling participants why certain skills are needed and what they are, is unlikely to engage personal involvement as successfully.

- *Goal-setting or further skills practice.* Encouragement to set goals or to make decisions about applying the learning can be offered in various ways. Many IST events conclude with a reflection and 'action-planning' activity, with the aim of helping participants to plan how they will apply what they have learned to clearly identified work situations. Alternatively, an opportunity can be provided to 'draw the learning together' by trying out new ideas in an experiential skills-practice activity.

Setting the learning process out as above may make it appear somewhat laborious or mechanical. However, each step can be achieved in a wide variety of ways, so workshop designs need not become repetitive – although it is also important to avoid switching confusingly between one type of exercise and another. The steps should flow from each other naturally, and often individuals will be involved in different ways at any one time (for example, depending on whether they are acting as observers or taking an active part). The most important point is that everyone has the opportunity to engage in all aspects of the cycle at some stage during the session, and that sufficient time is allocated for this to be possible. While staffing and other pressures can pose scheduling problems for IST, it should be recognized that very short events often cannot provide an adequate framework for 'whole-cycle' learning to take place, and if time is very limited, it is especially important that the trainer resists trying to pack too much into one session.

Learning transfer

Assuring successful transfer of learning from the training session to the workplace is often seen primarily as a matter of using exercises or examples which are as close to participants' 'real life' as possible. This is certainly important, and methods which can serve this purpose include full-scale organizational simulations and small-scale role-play scenarios. Group members can also be asked to work in various ways on organizational situations and problems that they have actually experienced, or are expecting to experience.

However, participants' work experience and training needs will not be uniform by any means, and it will not always be possible to involve everyone in experiential activities which directly reflect their outside experience. This should not be a problem as long as participants are always encouraged to consider the relevance of activities and other people's perspectives to their own work roles and experiences. Timing and follow-up of training, too, are all-important factors: transfer is more likely when what is learned can swiftly be put into practice back in the workplace. For instance, it would be less than ideal for someone to attend an event about chairing meetings effectively if there is a large time-lapse before the next time they have to do this. Likewise, action-planning and goal-setting at the end of a workshop may come to nothing if follow-up opportunities in some form are not available to the learner.

Learning preferences

While optimal learning occurs when people are able to engage skilfully in all aspects of the experiential learning cycle, in practice individuals tend to prefer some modes of learning over others, and gain particular benefits from these modes. Kolb's research led him to identify four different learning styles, according to the relative emphasis placed by individuals on the approaches to learning identified by the cycle. His learning style concepts have been popularized by Honey and Mumford, who have described them as 'activist', 'reflector', 'theorist' and 'pragmatist', each one corresponding to one of the stages of the learning cycle.[4] They are characterized as follows:

- *activists* enjoy becoming fully involved in new experiences and learning through interaction with others; they are comfortable with 'here-and-now' engagement in experiential training activities;
- *reflectors* prefer taking an observer role, and having time to assimilate experiences and consider ideas from a number of perspectives;
- *theorists* are analytical and appreciate the power of models, systems and theories in illuminating experience or aiding problem-solving;
- *pragmatists* enjoy 'hands-on' experimentation which is directly relevant to practical problem-solving.

Although these four 'types' are simplifications, IST participants are likely to respond with varying degrees of enthusiasm to the different parts of a workshop, and their responses may well reflect their particular learning styles and preferences. Some may be more comfortable than others with exercises involving practical experimentation – such as role-playing. Some may feel that the theoretical input is the most useful part of the session, while others may learn best when there is a very obvious connection between an activity and a 'real-life' situation at work. It is important to be aware of the variety of learning styles, and to cater for them, to ensure that participants have the opportunity to engage in activities they find most rewarding. Equally importantly, a balanced mix of activities, carefully facilitated, will help participants to develop their learning abilities and gain benefit from aspects of the programme to which they feel less attracted.

In some circumstances, a valuable preliminary to participation in IST is to introduce group members to the concept of different learning styles, and to invite them to analyse their own preferences, perhaps using the Learning Styles Questionnaire designed for that purpose. It is certainly useful at the start of an IST event to outline the types of activities which will be involved in the programme and to explain why they are being used. Developing personal awareness of learning preferences, strengths and weaknesses can lead individuals to become more committed to developing their learning skills and engaging in the programme as a whole.

It is also possible to tailor workshop designs to suit the preferences of participants, if these are known in advance, and sometimes this may be appropriate to the aims and objectives of the programme. Whole organizations, too, may develop a characteristic approach to learning as part of their culture, and this will influence the preferences of members. It is as well for trainers to be aware of this, and to remember that, as individuals, they too are likely to have learning preferences, which may bias their training designs or the emphasis they place on different aspects of the workshop.

Learning anxieties

As well as understanding how adults learn, it is important for IST trainers to be aware of factors that can 'get in the way' of learning. In particular, when feelings of anxiety outweigh learners' interest and enthusiasm, the potential to learn will be impaired. Quite understandably, many participants in IST bring some anxieties to a workshop, or feel uneasy in some way at points in the programme. For instance, if experiential learning methods are unfamiliar to them, or if they have had a negative IST experience in the past, they may feel uncomfortable at the prospect of carrying out a role-play and receiving feedback on their performance.

Others may feel wary about the training style to be adopted by the facilitator, or about his or her level of skill. Anxieties can arise about disclosing personal views and feelings, particularly if there are differences in organizational status among group members. The very subject-matter of interpersonal skills can feel threatening to many. Fears of embarrassment, exposure, disapproval or ridicule can be expressed by group members in a variety of ways (for instance, through cynicism, denial, hostility or withdrawal); whatever the case, trainers need to be able to read the signs of anxiety in participants' behaviour, and to help establish productive learning relationships and attitudes in the group.

IST trainers need therefore to recognize that their role is to manage the risk level in the group in order that learning is not blocked. Essentially, this means designing a programme and then establishing a group climate in which safety and challenge are equally balanced – so that participants feel able to take risks involved in trying out new activities or in expressing their views and feelings. Both too much and too little challenge experienced by group members will inhibit their learning.

3.4 Setting process aims and objectives

It should be clear from the discussion above of aids and blocks to learning that process aims relate to the need to plan for and, during the workshop, actively to facilitate a number of basic conditions which will encourage learning and its transfer to the workplace. Some examples of trainers' process aims are the following:

- to enable participants to take responsibility for their own learning;
- to provide opportunities for participants to: become fully involved in experiential activities; engage in personal reflection and give and receive feedback; identify general principles; practise skills and plan action;
- to establish a climate in the group in which participants will feel safe to take risks in their learning.

Process objectives are more precise formulations of how the process aims are to be achieved. Key skills involved in facilitating supportive, stimulating group-work for IST are outlined in Chapter 5. Workshop design principles which can help reduce the level of learning anxiety are outlined in Chapter 4.

References

1   Dainow, S. and Bailey, C., *Developing skills with people: training for person to person client contact*, Chichester, Wiley, 1988.
2   Knowles, M., *Androgogy in action*, (2nd edn), London, Jossey Bass, 1990.
3   Kolb, D. and Fry, R., 'Towards an applied theory of experiential learning', in Cooper, C. L. (ed.), *Theories of group process*, Chichester, Wiley, 1975.
4   Honey, P. and Mumford, A., *Using your learning styles*, (2nd edn), Maidenhead, Peter Honey, 1986.

 # Design of IST events

This chapter reviews basic elements of workshop design, focusing on the principles of structure, the choice of available methods and formats, and the preparation of workshop materials. It concludes with a sample workshop outline.

4.1   IST group composition and size

Whether IST groups should be composed of staff of the same or different grades and functions will depend on the learning objectives in question. 'Mixed' groups from one library service are useful when exchange of experience and perspectives from different parts of the library are important, and when exploration of common ground is needed. However, it is likely that disparities between the status of group members and closeness of hierarchical relationships will have an impact on the level of safety experienced by participants, and these factors will need to be taken into account in the course design.

In cases when only one trainer is to facilitate the group-work, it is generally accepted that optimum IST group size – for encouraging group members to relax and participate freely – is between eight and twelve members. The apparent economic gains to be made by using larger groups with a single trainer should be assessed carefully, since ultimate cost-effectiveness may well decrease with increased group size.

4.2   Workshop structure

IST workshops need a clear beginning, middle and end. Activities in the introductory part are mainly concerned with establishing group relationships and setting the tone for the participative and experiential work to come. The main body of the event includes all the activities through which the work gets done. A final session allows participants to review their learning, focus on the transition back to work and participate in the closure of the group.

4.2.1   Beginning of workshop

Making a comfortable and stimulating start to an IST workshop sets the foundations for the success of the programme as a whole. It is therefore extremely important to plan enough time and appropriate activities for this to be achieved; even if the trainer and some participants feel impatient to 'get down to the real work', cutting corners at this stage may well turn out to be counter-productive later on. The activities suggested below deal with a number of important introductory steps, and at the same time serve to familiarize group members with the style and philosophy of learning which is to be adopted for the rest of the workshop.

Trainer's introduction

It is usual for the trainer to begin by welcoming participants to the course and, if s/he is not known to them, to introduce her/himself. This will pave the way for participants to disclose something of themselves in their own introductions. They are likely to be interested in finding out something about the trainer's professional experience and interests, and it may be useful to explain how the trainer's involvement in this particular event came about. If in addition to providing factual information, s/he says something about her/his own feelings at the start of the workshop, participants may feel easier about referring to theirs.

Participants' introductions

The way participants' introductions are handled will depend on whether or not they know each other already, and if they do, to what extent. It should also be borne in mind that, for many, anticipating speaking to the whole group for the first time, and actually doing so, can be very stressful.

There are many formats for introductions. The example below is commonly used for participants who do not know each other, and there are numerous possible variations of it:

- Participants turn to the person sitting next to them and spend five minutes getting to know each other's name and something about each other. They then move on to meet another pair and use this information to introduce their partner to the others. Finally, the whole training group reconvenes and participants introduce their partner to everyone else.

When group members already know each other, introductions can be adapted accordingly. It can be left up to participants to decide what information they would like to give to introduce themselves, or the trainer can specify particular themes. For instance, participants might be asked to say something about their work roles, and something about some other aspect of their lives. They could simply describe something pleasant that has happened to them over the last 24 hours. Ideally, however, introductions should begin to focus minds on the workshop topic itself, and on a course which will engage people in personal-awareness work, they might be asked to say something about a personal view or feeling. For instance, a course on effective teamwork could begin by asking participants to reflect on and exchange information in pairs about what they enjoy about working in a team. The trainer should be included in the introductions to the whole group, by responding to the same questions asked of participants.

Group introductions are often known as 'ice-breakers' and can take the form of games instead of information-sharing. For instance, a widely used name game asks people to stand in a circle and to introduce themselves and each other by means of a cumulative 'group name round'. The first would introduce herself ('I'm Mary'); the second would introduce Mary and herself ('This is Mary and I'm Sue'); the third would introduce the two who have gone before and himself ('This is Mary, this is Sue and I'm Mike'); and so on.

The purpose of this type of exercise is to provide a light-hearted warm-up, and games can certainly serve to relax participants through laughter and some degree of physical activity if facilitated sensitively. However, some people dread such activities, and they should be used with caution. The likely risk level in the group should always be taken into account when planning to use such activities. Moreover, if the trainer does not feel comfortable at the prospect of facilitating a particular ice-breaker, it is advisable to select another one; any anxiety on her/his part could well communicate itself to participants, with negative consequences.

Introduction to programme and learning objectives

Group members should be made aware of the general aims of the workshop and its programme prior to taking part; it is a good idea to provide everyone with a written programme outline at least a couple of days in advance, if possible. It is important to re-introduce this at the start of the workshop, giving a brief overview of main themes and more detail about the mix of learning activities which will be involved.

This is also the time to invite participants to think about and communicate their personal learning objectives; this will encourage them to begin to take responsibility for their learning, and they will gain from hearing about the range of interests represented in the group. Usually a great deal of common ground emerges, as well as some differing perspectives. Discussion of learning objectives allows the trainer to clarify what is being offered to the group; it also gives him or her a chance to establish the extent to which the planned workshop is on course for meeting people's needs and expectations, and whether or not it will be necessary to make any adjustments. Sometimes some participants' interests do not coincide exactly with what has been planned or their expectations are unrealistic in some way, and it is important that everyone understands in advance what is on offer and what they can reasonably hope to gain from the course. If group members feel they do not have any clear learning objectives, it is worth explaining why it is useful to spend time thinking about what they want to get out of the workshop, and that this will enable them to evaluate it more clearly at the end. Some negotiation may need to take place in order to establish a satisfactory 'learning contract' between group members and the trainer.

Including an early opportunity for participants to express any concerns about learning methods or anything else to do with participating in the workshop, can do much to reassure. For example, unfounded fears of having to do a role-play in front of the whole group can be defused if participants are given the chance to express misgivings openly and are informed of the way in which such activities are to be organized. Of course, it is important to be honest: if the workshop is to include role-play in front of the whole group, then participants should be told, the rationale for it explained, and an indication given of whether or not everyone's participation is expected.

The trainer needs to be prepared for the possibility that open discussion of participants' aims and concerns may lead to the expression of negative feelings, such as resentment or upset about having been 'sent' on the workshop, or the conviction that it will be of little or no use. If this happens, it is a good opportunity to sort out some difficulties right from the start, and obviously the trainer should plan in advance the type of response s/he will wish to make. Having invited group members to express their aims and concerns, s/he must be prepared to respond to them directly and honestly.

For short workshops, discussion of learning objectives and concerns will be fairly brief, but on a longer programme, it is worth spending a reasonable amount of time on this process. A simple format is to ask group members to reflect individually for a few minutes on the two following questions, and to jot down their responses before feeding back, in turn, to the group:

- What do you hope to gain from attending the workshop?
- What concerns, if any, do you have about the workshop?

It is useful to make a note on a flip chart of what participants say, so that the themes and issues can be referred to during the workshop and, especially, at the end.

The scope of this exercise can be expanded in various ways, and it is worth considering the range of possible formats for discussion of personal concerns and feedback to the group. For instance, group members might think about the following questions:

- What will you need to do in order to achieve your learning aims?
- What might get in the way of your achieving your learning aims?
- What expectations do you have about the workshop?

It is not always necessary for personal responses to this type of question to be made public in the group. Participants could share some responses in pairs only, or keep some entirely to themselves. A way of reducing the level of risk would be to request that answers to the questions be written anonymously on cards, which can then be posted up on the wall for everyone to read.

Ground-rules for group-work

The type of activity described above, in raising the issue of group members' concerns, can also lead into discussion and establishment of an appropriate 'group contract' for the duration of the workshop. It is important that participants recognize their own and others' needs as group members, and understand that responsibility for maintaining a productive group climate with positive norms has to be shared between all members. Again, the amount of time spent on setting ground-rules for the group will depend on the length and topic of the workshop, but some attention will nearly always need to be paid to issues of trust and respect. Participants will naturally be more likely to contribute openly to discussions if they are confident that what they choose to say will not be reported by someone else outside the training event, or indeed outside the particular group format in which it is said. They will also be happier about participating if they are sure that they will be listened to respectfully by their fellow group members. Agreements about confidentiality and sensitivity to others' contributions should therefore be made, and there may well be a number of other issues that the trainer or other group members will wish to raise (such as 'permission' to make mistakes, responsibility for personal learning, guide-lines for giving constructive critical feedback, and so on). Some housekeeping arrangements may also need to be agreed, such as rules relating to smoking, punctuality and commitment to consistent attendance if the course is to take place over a number of weeks.

Ground-rules can emerge out of the discussion of aims and concerns described above, or a special activity can be undertaken to address these issues. A fairly extended group contract activity could take the following form:

- Following a brief explanation of group contracts by the trainer, triads are formed and each one supplied with a pile of blank sheets of paper. The triads conduct a 'brainstorm' activity for ten minutes, eliciting and recording personal responses to the statement: 'How I would like the group to be is ...'. Every response is noted down on a separate piece of paper. The group reconvenes and each one is displayed, explained if necessary, and agreement on it requested. Assuming agreement is reached (which may be after some discussion, and the trainer should always be careful to ensure that assent is universal) the sheets of paper are posted up on the wall in order to maintain a public record of each component of the group contract. The resulting full-scale contract remains visible throughout the workshop.

Housekeeping details

Finally, participants should be informed about practicalities such as the availability of handouts and arrangements for ensuring physical comfort. For instance, they will need to know the location of lavatories, times of planned breaks and type and location of meals and refreshments, what the possibilities are for requesting other short breaks if needed, or for making adjustments to room temperature.

4.2.2   Main body of workshop

The design task for the main body of an experiential IST workshop entails selecting a mix of learning methods and formats which will meet its content and process objectives, and then arranging activities into an appropriate sequence and time-frame.

Selection of learning activities

A range of common IST methods and formats is outlined below (section 4.3). General factors which need to be taken into consideration when selecting activities include the following:

- The need to offer a reasonable (but not overwhelming) variety of activities; this includes varying the length of sessions and using different media.
- The need to include opportunities for relaxation and fun. Breaks for refreshment should be long enough to allow participants to visit the lavatory if they wish, or to get some fresh air and stretch their legs. Other short breaks can be fitted into a programme; physical activities such as quick stretching exercises or, if acceptable to participants, lively games can help dispel tension and restore concentration. It is important to try to select games in which everyone can be included if they wish, although the trainer will always need to check whether or not everyone can join in with some games, for reasons of physical ability. Word-games are a quieter alternative. Participants can be invited to contribute suggestions for relaxation activities, and asking participants to lead games is a useful way of changing the leadership dynamic of the group for a while.
- Constraints on resources, for instance as regards time, technology, space, the ratio of trainers to group size.
- The value of building in ongoing personal reflection and evaluation. If the course is a fairly long one, it is useful to allow breaks for participants to reflect on the extent to which they are meeting their learning objectives, and to give the trainer feedback about the course design.

The activities selected will also depend on the trainer's own preferences and skills. While there is no reason not to experiment with some new methods on a programme, if the trainer is very uncomfortable facilitating any particular type of activity, this may well affect the quality of participants' experience. Team-training might be considered for these parts of the programme, with the trainer working alongside someone else who is more familiar with a certain method; this will contribute to the development of her/his own skills and will not deprive participants of the benefits of the method itself.

Sequence of activities

The following factors should be taken into account when planning the sequence of activities:

- Simpler concepts need to be introduced before more difficult ones, and some skills need to be introduced before others.
- Participants' prior knowledge and skills should be acknowledged and built upon. It may be tempting to start a programme with a presentation offering definitions of skills. However, in order to encourage participants to reflect on personal experience, assess their own level of knowledge and exchange different perspectives, it would be more useful to start by asking *them* to define the skills in question. This also gives the trainer an insight into the levels of knowledge and skills within the group.
- The logical stages of the experiential learning process, as identified in Chapter 3.
- The degree of risk that activities may represent for participants. There are a number of ways that the stress of risk can be reduced. First, unless the group is very familiar with experiential learning methods, it makes sense to start out with 'lower-risk' activities and to build up to 'higher risk' ones at a stage when personal confidence and group trust are likely to be better established. For instance, most people feel more able to cope with the challenge of receiving feedback from others after having the chance to consider their behaviour from their own point of view. Similarly, talking generally about their organization or their jobs can break the ice for talking subsequently at a more personal level (disclosing feelings, experiences or views). Because of very common fears of embarrassment, it would usually be a mistake to start a workshop with an activity involving a high degree of public personal experimentation, such as role-play. However, it is worth bearing in mind that what is experienced as threatening for one person may be less so for another, and vice versa. While some people will be happy with quite high levels of self-disclosure, others will be very unhappy.

    Thus, a 'personal sharing' exercise in pairs to evaluate teamwork in the library could invite participants to reflect on and discuss issues in the following sequence:

- Overall, the strengths I see in teamwork in the library are...
- Overall, the weaknesses I see in teamwork in the library are...
- The types of teamwork I am involved in are...
- My particular strengths in teamwork are...
- For me, the main difficulties in working in a team are...

Group members are likely to feel safer discussing what has happened in the past or what might occur in the future, than what is actually going on in the 'here and now'. For instance, it is easier for someone to receive feedback about how they have handled a difficult situation with a library user the week before the training event, than to receive feedback about their performance in the workshop itself in a role-play dealing with a 'difficult client'. Receiving feedback about their 'here-and-now' behaviour as a group member would be even more difficult. So workshops can be structured accordingly, with activities focusing on the past preceding those which explore the present.

Finally on this issue, the size of the group will affect the level of risk experienced by participants. For most people, the larger the group, the higher the risk. It is by no means necessary to conduct the whole of a workshop in one large group, and most activities are amenable to different formats, such as work in pairs, triads and so on. There can be advantages in working in larger groups (as when the aim is to explore the extent of variety in people's views), but it is usu-ally advisable to begin with smaller formats and to work up more gradually to full-group activities.

Planning the workshop timing

It can be difficult to estimate timings for IST activities, and they will vary according to the size, needs and interests of the group. Less experienced trainers often underestimate the amount of time that will be needed for experiential work, and attempt to fit too much into one session. Other fac-tors such as the time it takes to give instructions about activities, and the almost inevitable 'slippage' at the beginning of the workshop and after breaks, have to be taken into account. It will be important to finish punctu-ally to fit in with participants' other commitments and, in any case, concen-tration is likely to falter if a planned closing-time passes. With experience, timings do become easier to predict, and trainers may also feel more confi-dent about remaining flexible and perhaps making some adjustments to the plan during the workshop itself. If worried that participants will get through the programme faster than expected, the trainer can plan addi-tional activities as 'back-ups'; alternatively, if concerned that time will become tight, some activities can be identified as 'optional extras' which could be removed without altering the overall balance of the programme.

4.2.3 Close of workshop

The last part of the workshop should be planned to achieve the following:

- Review by participants of key themes and personal learning
- Consideration of follow-up actions and goal-setting
- Evaluative feedback about the workshop
- Closure of the group's 'life'.

Some suggestions for activities to meet these objectives are made below. There is no need to plan a separate activity to meet each one; a single activ-ity could easily be designed to meet them all at the same time. However, it is important that this consolidation part of the course is not rushed, and in particular that enough time is allocated to participants' personal reflection and forward-planning.

Personal learning review

Learning objectives identified at the start of the course are re-examined. Participants are asked to form pairs with the person with whom they initially discussed their objectives, and to answer the question: 'What have I gained from attending the course?' They then feed back this information to the whole group, as a 'group round'.

Another idea is to provide all participants with a 'Personal Learning Review' questionnaire, which they fill in individually and keep as a record of the workshop. An example of this type of instrument is given in Appendix 2.

Action planning and goal-setting

All participants write down two things they aim to do differently as a result of the course and share this information with a partner.

Alternatively, a 'group round' can be held on the topic of 'One idea that I will take back to work with me and try to implement'. It might also be appropriate to ask participants to think about forward-planning for follow-up training or self-development activities.

If the course has included work by each participant on a real-life problem they have in the library, this would be a good moment to reflect on the problem again and to review and record how they could use what they have learned on the course to manage the problem more effectively.

End-of-workshop feedback

Participants are asked to provide immediate, open-ended verbal feedback about their experience of the course, perhaps by answering questions such as 'The session I gained most from was...' or 'Something I would like to have been different was...'. Alternatively, if there is time, pairs or small groups are formed to review the programme session by session, summarizing their evaluation of each one for the whole group.

It is common for brief evaluation forms to be handed out at the end of a workshop, and participants asked either to fill them in there and then, or to return them to the trainer within a short time-frame. The forms can be designed in a variety of ways: for instance, using open-ended or multiple-choice questions, or scaled measures. An example of an IST course evaluation form is given in Appendix 3.

This type of feedback is valuable insofar as it offers an insight into immediate satisfaction levels among participants, and might well be used to make important adjustments to the programme design. However, as far as longer-term behavioural impact is concerned, the information provided in this way is of very limited use to the trainer and, indeed, to the library management. Methods of evaluating change in performance, and of assessing ultimate benefits to the organization, are reviewed in Chapter 6.

Closing round

In order to mark the end of the group, it is useful to finish with a closing round in which everyone participates in the group one last time. Trainers have the choice of whether to ask group members to contribute in their own time, or systematically in turn around the group.

4.3 IST methods

Widely used learning methods for IST are briefly outlined below, and some indications are given about the preparation and implementation techniques they require. Suggestions for further reading on all the methods are given in the resource list (Appendix 1).

Self-concept instruments

These are generally pen-and-paper questionnaires or check-lists which participants use to assess their own, or their group's, interpersonal attitudes and behaviour. They are useful for awareness-raising or value clarification, and might exemplify aspects of a particular theory of communication; for example, a questionnaire might explore participants' assertiveness by asking them to identify their likely choice of behaviour in a variety of circumstances and assigning an assertiveness rating to overall scores. Some instruments ask participants to evaluate the behaviour of other individuals in the group.

As 'personality tests', the reliability and validity of such instruments are inevitably open to question, and so results derived from them should not be interpreted too literally; it is certainly unhelpful if participants unquestioningly accept their own scores as definitive descriptions of themselves or fall victim to stereotyping by others. Trainers should beware of overgeneralizing their accuracy, and some may feel that their failure to link behavioural concepts to social context places severe limitations on their value. However, as a stimulus for more interactive, nuanced exploration, they can be effective. Filling in a questionnaire is usually experienced as a relatively low-risk activity since feedback from it comes from the individuals themselves rather than from others, and personal scores need not necessarily be made public in the group.

Trainer presentations

Most experiential IST designs will include some lecturing input from the trainer, usually about aspects of relevant theory or research. Listening to lectures is often a rather passive activity; perhaps the most important point about trainer presentations for IST is that they should be made as lively and interactive as possible. Delivering an interactive lecture effectively is a matter of some skill; the following basic principles are a good start:

- The content must be directly related to the training objectives, and to participants' own work situations.
- Most learners have a fairly short attention span for taking in information in this way, so lectures should be kept brief (not more than 30 minutes).
- Lectures should have a clear structure, starting with an introduction which states what is to be covered, and ending with a conclusion which summarizes what has been said.
- The argument or exposition should develop logically, with different points supported by clear and relevant visual aids (people remember less of what they hear than of what they see).
- Wherever possible, points should be illustrated with concrete examples, rather than left as generalizations. A good idea is to invite participants to supply their own examples during the presentation.
- Active communication with the group should be maintained through eye contact and verbal responses to participants' reactions. This means that ideally notes should be used as a reference only (rather than read verbatim) and that, if an overhead projector is used, the trainer should beware of looking backwards at the screen.
- The input can be interrupted every now and then, for the trainer and

participants to ask questions or make comments. Participants can form small 'buzz groups' in which they discuss their reactions to the points that have been made.

- Handouts may be given out before, during or after the lecture, and serve different purposes accordingly. If distributed and read by participants beforehand, they can be used to lead into the lecture and provide the basis for group discussion; if distributed during the lecture, they can break it up and encourage participants' active involvement; if distributed afterwards, they act as reinforcement and reminders. Participants should be told whether or not handouts will be provided to support the lecture, so that they can make informed decisions about whether or not to take notes.

Video presentations and 'triggers'

Video programmes portraying human relations scenarios are frequently used in IST to provide extended cases or brief vignettes for analysis and discussion, as well as 'how to do it' and 'how not to do it' skills demonstrations. An approach widely used is to show the negative consequences of inadequate interpersonal behaviour (whether for organizational effectiveness or for relationships between colleagues and with clients), and then to illustrate how the situation could be better handled by using more effective interpersonal techniques. 'Trigger' videos typically present a series of very brief scenarios illustrating difficult one-to-one interactions culminating in a moment of crisis or communication failure; in some cases, the on-screen action is addressed directly to the viewer as one of the protagonists in the encounter. Watching the trigger scenario is followed up by exploration of participants' reactions, and discussion of possible solutions to the problem. Numerous commercially produced videos are available on a wide range of interpersonal and communication topics, and some have been produced specifically for use in libraries.

Some trainers feel that over-reliance on the positive and negative models portrayed by IST videos serves to encourage passivity on the part of learners, and can promote mechanistic or generalized versions of skilled behaviour. Positive models may not be relevant to participants' own perspectives or experience, and some learners may have difficulty differentiating between good and bad practice, or may identify so closely with negative models that the learning experience becomes stressful. In addition, skills are not unfailingly portrayed expertly by the actors on video. The following points are worth bearing in mind when using video presentations:

- Materials should be selected carefully, in order to ensure that they will be relevant to the experience and needs of participants. A video produced primarily for workers in non-library organizations may well transfer successfully to a library setting, but this cannot be assumed; its version of organizational life and of skilled behaviour could be at odds with participants' work experience and with the management styles or organizational cultures of their libraries.
- Prescriptive approaches to using video demonstrations are to be avoided. Participants should be encouraged to define skills on the basis of their own experience and needs rather than to accept 'imported' definitions uncritically. Video demonstrations are especially useful for stimulating personal reflection and discussion, and for reinforcing or consolidating experiential understanding, rather than as definitive stand-alone 'models' of skilled behaviour.

- As with trainer presentations, every effort should be made to implement the video session as interactively as possible, by building in plenty of opportunities for participants to discuss reactions, make comments and ask questions.

Group discussions

Group discussions enable participants to exchange views, ask questions and debrief following an experiential exercise. They can be held at any point during a workshop, in a variety of formats. For instance:

- *Large-group* discussions can be held in the whole training group, which is likely to consist of between eight and fourteen members. Generally, the more people in the group, the less likely it is that everyone will participate, and the more superficial the discussion will be. However, if facilitated sensitively, large group discussions can serve some purposes reasonably well.
- *Syndicate groups* are groups of between five and eight people who meet to discuss a particular question or issue; often, one member is elected to report the gist of the group's discussion to the others in a subsequent plenary session.
- A *'fishbowl'* group is observed by another, non-participating group while it holds a discussion. The fishbowl group sits in an inner circle surrounded by members of the observing group, and the fishbowl discussion is followed by debriefing about the process by both groups together.
- *'Buzz groups'* of three or four people are intended as brief, immediate opportunities for participants to share reactions to a point which has been made, or to something that has happened. They can be formed very quickly, last for up to ten minutes, and may lead into more general discussion in a larger group.

The following points are important for facilitating group discussion:

- The group will need a clear focus for the discussion and an understanding of what it is to achieve. These can be provided by posing a question, asking the group to develop a list of points or criteria, or to share personal experiences.
- The group will need to know how much time it has to hold the discussion.
- Sitting in a circle is likely to encourage participation, and each group should have sufficient space to avoid becoming distracted by other discussions being held in the same room.

Brainstorming

Brainstorming is a participative technique for generating ideas quickly in a group. For instance, the trainer might ask for as many suggestions as possible for tackling a particular problem, or say: 'What are the skills involved in dealing effectively with criticism from users?' Participants are encouraged to call out whatever comes to mind, and every contribution is recorded and displayed, perhaps on a flip chart. In order to encourage creative thinking and uninhibited participation, it is important that while ideas are still being generated, they are not debated or assessed. Only after the brainstorm are the ideas explained, discussed and evaluated.

Guided fantasy

This is a method which aims to promote personal reflection and aware-ness-raising. The trainer asks participants to relax, close their eyes, and listen to a 'story' or a description of a situation in which participants are addressed as the protagonist. The story ends with a direct question, encouraging the listeners to explore the feelings and thoughts that the story has stimulated in them.

For instance, a guided fantasy might be used to raise participants' awareness of their attitudes to different user groups. The story begins with a description of the librarian getting up in the morning, having breakfast, travelling to work, and taking his or her place at the enquiry desk. The librarian is described watching users come through the door and disperse around the library. Some users approach the desk and make enquiries. The story ends by asking participants what type of user they have 'seen' in their imaginations as the story has unfolded: for instance, who has seen users who are male, female, black, white, disabled, old, young, etc.? The exercise is followed by a debriefing discussion in which participants consider the reasons for and implications of what they have and have not seen during the fantasy.

Case studies

An IST case study is a description of a human relations situation in an organizational setting. Cases are usually written, but also may be presented audiovisually. They raise a number of communication issues and a problem which usually can be tackled in a number of ways, providing a means of developing participants' problem-solving, analytical and decision-making skills. If the aim is to develop participants' diagnostic skills, the narrative does not state the real problem directly, but contains clues to it. Some learners find case studies particularly valuable when there are very close parallels between the case and their own work situations, but cases are useful for exploring general principles too, relating theory to practice.

Case studies must be directly relevant to the training objectives, realistic and sufficiently detailed and multi-faceted to stand in-depth analysis; plots can be based on real-life (personal or second-hand) library work experience, characters should be credible rather than stereotypical, and background information should be up-to-date. Such case studies can be time-consuming to research and write, and developing effective extended cases requires a fairly high level of skill. Briefer scenarios can also work well for some purposes; some examples of short cases are given in Appendix 4.

Case studies are generally used as the basis for group discussion, and groups can be asked to reach majority or consensus decisions about the way the problem should be tackled. They can be given as 'homework', to be read individually before discussion at the next session, and can also be used to lead into role-play or simulation exercises in which participants adopt the roles of different characters and explore the skills involved in solving interpersonal problems between them.

Role-play

This method invites participants to adopt the roles of people involved in interpersonal situations which parallel those experienced at work. It offers the chance to break out of patterns of inappropriate or ineffective behaviour, and to try out new approaches to difficult encounters. Role-play is a particularly powerful means of developing interpersonal skills, since it enables learners to practise their skills in situations which, although artificial in one sense, directly engage participants' feelings, attitudes and thoughts. Thus, whereas the case-study method is likely to stimulate mainly cognitive learning, role-play offers the potential for affective and behavioural learning as well. The importance of the debriefing session which is held after the role-play itself cannot be over-emphasized, and sufficient time should always be allocated to it.

As well as offering the chance to practise new skills in a relatively 'safe' environment, in which making mistakes will not much matter, role-play offers opportunities for experiencing interactions from unfamiliar points of view. Role-reversal (in which participants play both sides of an interaction in turn, or adopt the role of a real person who poses some kind of difficulty to them), can help participants to become more sensitive to the feelings of others, and to develop a more empathic approach to difficult or conflictual situations. Role-play also offers opportunities to non-players to analyse interactions closely through observation. Usually the method is used for one-to-one interactions, but scenarios with more characters can be devised.

Role-plays can be organized in a number of different ways, with options for paired work, small-group work and large-group formats, and for feedback derived from observers or audiovisual recordings. In general, it is important that players receive feedback from at least one observer, as well as from each other, so triads offer a useful low-risk structure. Participants may consider performing in front of a larger group too stressful – especially to begin with – but larger formats lend themselves to more intensive observation and feedback. Single-group formats give the facilitator more control in focusing the debriefing session, and in intervening in the action at appropriate moments if thought useful.

Pre-planned scenarios Players are each given a written briefing describing the situation from the point of view of the character whose role they are to adopt. Ample time should be given for them to read it through and think about the major characteristics of their role. In some cases, both players read the two briefings before they embark on the role-play. However, since in real life two people are likely to see a situation from different perspectives, and to have different information about factors affecting it, it is often more useful if players do not see the other character's briefing. If the scenario or the objectives of the characters are fairly complex, it can be helpful for role-players to prepare by discussing with an observer its major features and the strategy they intend to adopt before embarking on the role-play interaction itself.

- For instance, one player adopts the role of a recently recruited library assistant with problems outside work which are having an impact on his or her work performance. The other player adopts the role of the supervisor, who aims to talk to the assistant, find out what the problem is and come to an agreement with him or her about improving work behaviour. After reading through their respective briefings and identifying the major points that need to be conveyed, the couple play out the conversation.

Scenarios for pre-planned role-play are not difficult to devise as long as some basic principles are borne in mind:

- Situations should be selected which are relevant to the training objectives, and which reflect the needs and experience represented in the group. With training groups composed of different categories of staff, it will not always be possible to devise scenarios which closely match everyone's experience, but it should be possible to select 'generic' situations with which all group members can identify.
- When writing a role-play scenario, it is useful to start by identifying the interpersonal skills which should be used by the players and the learning points that the activity should generate. The scenario can then be built up around these factors.
- As with case studies, role-play scenarios and characters should be credible and non-stereotypical. They should be neither too complex nor too simplistic. Enough detail should be given for players to develop their roles without excessive need for improvisation, although it is usually appropriate to encourage some improvisation.
- Where appropriate, role briefings should include clear instructions about the characters' aims in the interaction; for instance, an active listening briefing might state: 'Your aim is to find out as much as possible about the situation from your partner's point of view'.

Real-life scenarios   In general, the more closely participants can relate to the role-play scenario, the richer the learning is likely to be. Players can be asked to describe real-life scenarios to their role-play partner (which may be situations they have already experienced, or are expecting to experience in the future) and then the pair act out the situation together. Naturally, it is important that players are not pressured into disclosing details of a real-life situation which they would prefer to keep to themselves.

- For instance, a participant (A) describes a problematic encounter that has occurred with a library user, explaining the user's 'difficult' behaviour, and his or her own response. The role-play partner (B) adopts the user's role, enabling A to try a different approach to dealing with the situation from the one she or he had previously adopted. Alternatively, the roles can be swapped, B adopting A's role, which gives A the chance to experience the situation from the user's point of view, and to see how someone else (B) might handle it. This can be a very effective format, since the person who experienced the situation in the first place knows specifically what type of behaviour she or he was confronted with, and so can make the role-play more true to life. In addition, sometimes players understandably become stuck when trying to deal differently with a situation that has presented real problems for them, or which they greatly fear, and someone else's approach can be enlightening.

Observer and feedback briefings   As well as role briefings, it is advisable to prepare observer and feedback briefings to support the activity, such as the following:

- Written briefings for observers should indicate what they should be looking out for during the role-play and perhaps offer them a framework for recording their observations.
- If role-play is to be conducted in small groups, guide-lines about how participants should tackle the feedback and debriefing session will be needed. Written guide-lines may be used to reinforce a previous

activity in which feedback criteria have been negotiated within the training group. Debriefing should offer ample opportunity for personal reflection, and all feedback should be constructive (non-judgemental, descriptive rather than evaluative, and both positive and critical). Players should have the opportunity to explore their own feelings and to exchange feedback with each other before receiving feedback from observers and then from the trainer.

- Audiovisual recordings are an effective means of monitoring. If used, guide-lines can be prepared to help focus players' and observers' analysis of the recording.

Facilitation guidelines   Because participants may associate role-play with distressing learning experiences, it is important that sessions are facilitated sensitively. The following strategies are useful:

- Role-play sessions should be introduced by an explanation of their purpose, and what will be involved for all those taking part. If the trainer intends to circulate between small groups, watching and perhaps intervening in ('freezing') the action, participants should be prepared for this and understand why it is being done.
- Participants should be reassured that the aim is not to produce a seamless performance, but to explore a situation and to practise skills. The trainer can indicate to them that if the interaction seems to be going in the wrong direction, they can always stop the action and take some 'time out' to debrief and use each other and the observer to think about alternative strategies.
- If some participants are very anxious, it can be suggested that they take the role of observer before engaging actively in a role-play.
- Following the role-play, participants should have the chance to express their feelings about it before moving on to discussion of learning points.
- Trainer feedback should be descriptive rather than evaluative, and the debriefing session should explore the variety of participants' reactions and views and offer suggestions rather than prescriptive formulae from the trainer.

An example of role briefings for a pre-planned role-play is given in Appendix 5.

Simulations
Simulations are more elaborate forms of role-play, in which a particular organizational setting or situation is replicated in the training room and a number of players are involved in a series of interactions. For instance, an hour in the life of the library enquiry desk could be enacted, with participants taking the roles of users, reference librarians and colleagues. At intervals, the trainer stops the activity for reflection and debriefing sessions. Clearly, this type of activity is complex and requires a good deal of careful planning and preparation with the group; if time and resources are available (and it is likely that more than one trainer will be needed), it can be most effective.

Skills practice exercises
These are usually one-to-one exercises which enable participants to isolate and systematically to practise one core skill, or a small range of core skills.

For instance, participants could be asked to practise paraphrasing and summarizing in the following way:

- Participants form pairs, adopting the roles of A and B. A speaks without interruption for a minute or so about a difficult encounter she or he has experienced recently with a library user. After a while, A stops speaking and B paraphrases what has been said. A gives B feedback about the accuracy of the paraphrase, and if necessary B amends it until it is accepted as accurate. A continues speaking and the same process is repeated four or five times. Finally, B summarizes the whole of what A has said, and the accuracy of the summary is also debriefed. Then A and B swap roles, so that A is able to practise his or her skills in the same way.

IST Games

IST games are practical tasks which participants undertake in groups or pairs, with the aim of achieving a specified goal; the activity might involve negotiating, competing or collaborating. As with role-play and simulations, the debriefing following the game is a crucial part of the whole process, when the focus is on the interpersonal process by which the game was conducted.

- For instance, a game called 'Broken Squares' on the theme of group cooperation requires participants to form small groups which compete against each other to arrange cut-out shapes in squares – rather like jigsaws – as fast as possible. The groups play according to different rules governing the way members are able to communicate and each group has one or two observers. Following the game, the interpersonal dynamics of each group are reviewed in relation to its performance, and the style and performance of the different groups compared.[1] There are many sources of IST games on the market, or it is possible to develop one's own to suit particular training objectives.

4.4 Learning formats

Having selected the methods for the workshop, the appropriate format for each activity needs to be chosen. Some methods require particular formats, but most can be organized in a number of ways. The following options are available:

- individual work
- paired work
- small-group work (three to five members)
- large-group work (six members or more)
- inter-group work (such as the 'fishbowl' structure outlined above).

4.5 Workshop materials

The next step is to select or prepare materials to support the chosen IST activities. The following are likely to be required.

Materials for participants

- Resources to support experiential activities, for instance written role-play or case-study scenarios, video presentations, questionnaires, process instructions, etc.
- Handouts to reinforce key learning points.

Materials for trainer

- Overhead projection transparencies to support lecturing input
- An outline of the workshop design and content. Less experienced trainers will probably include more detail in their personal notes than more experienced trainers
- A file of 'masters' of all materials to be used on the workshop, supplemented by masters of any further materials which would support alternative activities if required.

Selecting and designing resources

At present, the range of up-to-date, commercially available IST materials which are tailored directly to library use, and which are of a high standard, is limited. However, although it would be helpful if more 'off-the-shelf' resources of this type were available, the current state of affairs should not be seen as too great an obstacle to providing high-quality library IST. Since it is vital that materials selected for any IST course are directly relevant to its training objectives and to the particular library environment, it is often necessary to develop materials in-house, or to adapt what is available from elsewhere. The task of developing or customizing materials is creative and rewarding, and excellent results can be achieved at reasonable cost; the more experience the trainer has, the faster the task can be accomplished. Some suggestions for producing IST materials have been made in the section above, and there are many manuals which offer more detailed guidance. In addition, many guides to IST include examples of skills practice activities, structured exercises and 'masters' for handouts which can be used for library IST with little or no adaptation; a small selection of these is included in Appendix 1.

Since many library trainers and working groups develop resources in-house, it makes sense to form cooperative arrangements for swapping ideas and IST materials. In addition, while it may seem preferable to draw directly on library-oriented materials, it may well be more productive to tap into the rich supplies of resources which support IST for other sectors. More expensive commercially produced items – of which there is no shortage – can be purchased jointly by training cooperatives, or may be available via the central training unit of the library's parent organization, which may also be able to provide help in producing materials for the library itself. Much material produced for other sectors (whether public, private or voluntary) will need to be adapted for library settings, but many ideas are directly transferable. Appendix 1 indicates a number of commercially available library IST materials, and sources of materials produced for other types of organization.

4.6 Sample workshop design

The following is an example of what an IST workshop might look like.

People Under Pressure
Interpersonal skills for effective library service

Aims

The workshop has been designed in response to reports from all grades of library staff of difficulties in dealing with criticism and complaints from users, resulting from increased pressures on the library service and some recent changes in policy. The workshop aims to give participants an opportunity to work together to identify and practise interpersonal skills which are helpful for handling stressful encounters of this type effectively. It should be equally useful as an introduction to the topic for some staff, and as a refresher course for others.

Objectives

The course will enable participants to:

* Reflect on and analyse personal experiences of stressful encounters with users
* Identify and list helpful interpersonal skills for dealing with these types of situation, focussing especially on dealing with criticism and complaints
* Participate in skills-practice exercises in active listening and assertiveness, applying these skills to a user criticism or complaint scenario
* Assess personal strengths in these skill areas, and areas for further development.

Programme

9.15   <u>Start of workshop</u>

<u>Trainer's introduction</u>

<u>Group introductions and 'ice-breaker'</u>
Group splits into pairs, to think about and exchange information on what they find enjoyable about working directly with users.
Group reconvenes and participants introduce themselves and feed back an enjoyable aspect of their work.

<u>Trainer's introduction to workshop aims and outline</u>

<u>Group aims and concerns</u>
Participants reflect individually on (a) what they want to get out of the workshop and (b) what, if anything, they have concerns about.
Responses are written on cards and posted on wall.

<u>Trainer-led debriefing</u>
Aims and concerns and establishment of ground-rules.
Housekeeping information given.

10.00	**Difficult situations with users**
	Activity in pairs. Each participant identifies and describes one difficult situation s/he has experienced recently, considering specifically: (a) what it was that made the situation difficult and stressful; (b) how s/he dealt with it; and (c) what was needed to deal with it effectively.
	Feedback from activity and trainer input
	Common difficulties and views on skills and other factors identified; value of listening and assertiveness highlighted.
11.00	**Coffee break**
11.15	**Defining active listening**
	Small-group brainstorm activity.
	Feedback from brainstorms and trainer input
	Verbal and non-verbal active listening skills discussed and listed.
12.15	**Active listening practice**
	Exercise in pairs. Identification of barriers to active listening and opportunity to practise skills. Debriefing in pairs and feedback from partner on skills.
12.45	**Lunch break**
1.45	**Defining assertiveness**
	Large-group brainstorm activity and trainer input.
	Dealing assertively with complaints and criticism
	Case-study activity in small groups. Groups discuss prepared cases and compile list of suggestions for dealing with them.
	Assertiveness techniques
	Feedback from group discussions and trainer input.
3.15	**Tea break**
3.30	**Using the skills**
	Role-play activity in groups of three. Participants work either on personal scenarios identified in morning, or on prepared scenarios, to practise active listening and assertiveness techniques for dealing with criticism and complaints.
4.30	**Trainer-led debriefing in whole group**
5.00	**Personal learning review and course evaluation**
	Self-assessment/reflection activity on what has been gained from the workshop and how it can be applied, personal strengths and areas for further development.

<u>Closing round</u>
Evaluation of workshop

5.30   <u>Close of workshop</u>

Reference

1   Adapted from 'Squares' in Bond, T., *Games for social and life skills*, London, Hutchinson, 1986, 216–19.

5 Delivery of training

At this stage, the role of the IST trainer is to help the training group meet its objectives by monitoring its progress and taking on leadership of the group. S/he has overall responsibility for establishing and maintaining a climate which is conducive to experiential learning, and for keeping the group-work focused and on course. In other words, s/he needs to be skilled in facilitating the group process of the workshop and in ensuring that the task gets done. Communication skills needed by the IST trainer can be grouped in two categories, according to whether they are associated with maintaining an appropriate group climate, or with ensuring the task is carried out. Both task and maintenance skills are required if a group is to function effectively. Key factors involved in playing this dual role successfully are outlined briefly in the following sections, and further reading on facilitation skills is indicated in Appendix 1. Facilitation skills and procedures specific to different learning activities are covered in Chapter 4 of the Guide.

5.1 Ensuring the task gets done

Task skills needed by the trainer include the following interpersonal strategies:

- *Initiating*. Contributions which start the group-work off are not only important at the beginning of the workshop, but may be necessary at other times when the direction needs to be changed.
- *Giving information*. This is done through scheduled inputs in the form of presentations, or less formally in the course of the workshop; it is important to achieve an appropriate balance between giving too much and too little.
- *Task-oriented questioning*. The trainer may need to help the group focus on and better define the task, or to find different ways of approaching it, by asking questions which challenge assumptions that have been made.
- *Clarifying*. By asking questions or paraphrasing, the trainer encourages participants to make general statements more specific, perhaps by using examples, and to identify the links between different members' contributions.
- *Summarizing*. The trainer often needs to conclude a discussion or session by summarizing the central points or helping the group to see what it has achieved before moving on to the next activity. Summarizing is useful when a group seems to have become stuck or lacks direction.
- *Timekeeping*. Participants should be informed of time-limits for activities, and it is the trainer's responsibility to ensure that enough – but not too much – time is allocated for each phase of the workshop.

5.2 Facilitating the group's process

The climate of an IST workshop is affected by numerous factors, including the nature of the physical environment, the changing feelings, attitudes and energy levels of individual participants, and relationships between them. Chapter 4 identified a number of ways in which workshop design can help to establish and maintain the necessary balance between safety and challenge in the group – so that participants feel sufficiently secure and sufficiently motivated to become fully involved in the learning process. Once the training is under way, the task is essentially the same – to continue to promote this balance, by supporting group members to take the risks involved in participating actively in the group-work, and by helping them to overcome any blocks to learning.

The physical environment
Generally accepted standards of physical comfort – relating to light, temperature, space, etc. – obviously need to be met if IST participants are to be able to work effectively. The arrangement of the room is also crucial, contributing much to setting the tone of the workshop right from the start, as well as to affecting the nature of participation once it gets going. A circular seating arrangement most strongly signals equality and intimacy between participants and trainer, and most easily promotes informal discussion. However, a horseshoe arrangement with the trainer sitting in a central position at the front is also effective, and makes using visual aids easier. The most important point is that group members and trainer all have a clear view of each other, so that direct communication between everyone is possible. Sometimes the trainer will need to ask participants to move their seats slightly in order to ensure that this is possible.

The trainer's style
The tone of the workshop is also set by the behaviour and appearance of the trainer. While in time a group may establish its own identity, at the start of a workshop participants form quick judgements about the trainer's credibility, and about the likely quality and nature of the training, according to the way in which s/he establishes her/his personal style. In many ways, the trainer acts as a behavioural model for participants, contributing to the establishment of group norms and demonstrating effective interpersonal skills. Although it is important that s/he clearly has expertise to offer, this does not mean that s/he has to convey the persona of infallible expert (which would almost certainly be counter-productive to the group's learning); however, the conduct of her/his interactions with participants does need to be consistent with the principles of effective communication being taught in the workshop and with the principles of participative working relations which s/he expects others to uphold.

In other words, IST trainers need to be able to practise what they preach, for instance by demonstrating appropriate self-disclosure and 'risk-taking'. If they are able to invite and accept personal feedback from participants about reactions to the workshop, and share some personal feelings with the group, this helps set the tone for everyone else. If the trainer is honest about personal strengths and weaknesses, and any questions to which s/he does not know the answer, this will help create an atmosphere of openness and shared learning.

The trainer's development of appropriate facilitation style will be helped if s/he has some knowledge of leadership theory. S/he can then make informed choices between leadership styles, based on an understanding of their likely effects on group development and learning. A well-known model of leadership identifies three common styles, known as 'democratic, authoritarian and laissez-faire'.[1] Democratic leadership style, which provides a structure within which all participants can take part in learning and decision-making, is most appropriate for the approach to IST described in this Guide. However, the trainer should be flexible and bring other styles to bear when appropriate to the needs of particular group circumstances.

Above all, however, as group leader it is important that the trainer relaxes as much as possible and develops confidence in her/his own style and personality, as well as awareness of areas for improvement. This may be easier said than done, particularly if s/he feels nervous in the role, or allows the example of other trainers to inhibit the development of her/his own style. With experimentation and experience, it should be possible to develop an effective style which feels natural. Certainly any lack of genuineness on the trainer's part will be detected speedily by participants and is likely to make them uneasy.

Group maintenance skills

Maintenance skills used by the trainer include the following:

- *Active listening.* The trainer needs to encourage equal participation and self-expression from group members, which may involve drawing attention to imbalances in levels of involvement. The verbal and non-verbal skills of active listening are vital here, such as the use of silence, paraphrasing and asking open questions. A good sense of timing is important for knowing when to intervene and when to remain silent to let participants reflect, or to let others contribute. In successful learning groups, participants communicate spontaneously and directly with each other as well as with the trainer.

  The ability to empathize is also important, in order that the trainer recognizes and responds appropriately and sensitively to individual participants' differing needs.

- *Challenging and feedback.* When there is conflict between participants, the trainer may need to mediate, encouraging communication between those involved and suggesting new ways of looking at the issue. The skills of active listening and challenging come into play here. There also may be times when the trainer needs to challenge inappropriate or restrictive behaviours and attitudes in the group. Sexism and racism are examples of such attitudes; alternatively, it may be that a participant's behaviour is disturbing the group's progress or inhibiting the participant's own learning (e.g. through withdrawal, aggression, domination of the discussion, etc.). It can be necessary to provide the whole group with feedback (or 'process observations') about the way it is functioning. For instance, this might be when only a few members are participating, or when the group is involved in 'taking sides'. Process observations draw attention to what is going on, so that the situation can be evaluated and the group dynamic improved.

  Challenging should always be done in a way which remains supportive and respectful of the person, while drawing attention to unacceptable or counter-productive behaviours or attitudes. Skills associated with challenging include assertiveness, giving constructive feedback, asking direct questions, and appropriate self-disclosure (sharing of personal feelings or experience).

- *Supporting*. The trainer needs to convey warmth and appreciation to participants, by offering positive (motivational) feedback and encouragement. Non-verbal behaviour is important here (nodding, smiling, etc.) as well as verbal appreciations of points and efforts made by participants.
- *Providing light relief*. Relaxation and release of tension within the group can be achieved through the use of humour, and a general atmosphere of fun will help learning to take place.
- *Communicating energy*. This is important for motivating participants; skills include making eye contact, speaking loudly and clearly, varying the tempo and pitch of the voice, and using expressive gestures.
- *Sharing personal experience (self-disclosure)*. This does not have to be of an intimate nature, but genuinely and directly communicates something relevant to an issue the group is working on. The value of appropriate self-disclosure in this context is that it helps others to feel safe in sharing their own experience, and therefore to relate personally and more deeply to the issue.

Dealing with difficult participants and groups

IST manuals sometimes present stereotypes of 'difficult participants', and offer advice on how to deal with such people. Usually what is meant by this is behaviour which is difficult for the trainer to handle (because s/he may feel criticized or undermined), or which inhibits the group's progress in some way. It should be clear from the description of trainer skills above, how their use applies to different types of group and participant behaviour which in some way blocks or inhibits learning or the group life. The important point is that the trainer develops her/his awareness of the types of behaviours to which s/he finds it most difficult to respond and develops her/his skills accordingly, avoiding being defensive and becoming embroiled in competitive arguments with participants. If a stage is reached where the group is not working at all well, it is important to call a halt and spend time looking at the reasons why.

It is useful if the trainer is able to place 'difficult' participant behaviour in the context of common patterns in group dynamics. Groups develop lives and personalities of their own, and some knowledge of group theory enables the facilitator to recognize and adequately respond to disruptive forms of group behaviour. A model of group behaviour which is very commonly described in IST manuals and communication textbooks identifies four stages of development (known as 'forming, storming, norming and performing').[2] Groups which develop in this way move (usually sequentially) from: anxiety and dependence on the leader; to internal conflict and rebellion against the leader's control; to increasing cooperation and the establishment of accepted norms; to participative task-oriented activity.

| 5.3 | Co-training |

There are many advantages to sharing the leadership of IST groups between two trainers. Co-trainers share responsibilities between them and, ideally, complement each other in style and skills. It is very important that co-trainers are aware of, and feel at ease with, each other's style, and plan the way they will lead the workshop carefully, so that their approaches are not in conflict.

5.4 Personal development and training for IST trainers

Training and personal development for trainers should be a continuous process, with plenty of opportunity to review and evaluate performance. All those involved in designing and delivering IST will benefit from ongoing training, including line managers and supervisors who have responsibility for coaching staff on-the-job as well as staff in full-time training posts and those with responsibility for training alongside their other duties.

In order to gain first-hand understanding of the learning process, and to support continued development of their own interpersonal skills, IST trainers need ongoing experience of IST as group participants. A foundation in basic counselling skills is particularly helpful for developing expertise in IST group facilitation, partly because of the need to be equipped to deal with both the inhibiting and enhancing effects of feelings on group learning processes; other forms of ongoing personal development such as assertiveness training and those which help with stress management (including personal therapy) are also useful. Attending IST events as a participant is also an excellent way of picking up new training ideas and gaining exposure to different trainer styles.

A number of library 'train-the-trainer' courses for IST design and facilitation are offered by the professional associations and by independent consultants, and outside the library world there is no shortage of relevant training providers. In addition, joint training arrangements may allow in-house trainers to work alongside trainers from the parent organization or elsewhere, as a means of developing skills for new topic areas.

References

1   See Dainow, S. and Bailey, C., *Developing skills with people: training for person to person client contact*, Chichester, Wiley, 1988.
2   Tuckmann, B. W., 'Developmental sequences in small groups', *Psychological bulletin*, **63** (6), 1965, 384–99.

 **Evaluating the training**

6.1 Forms of evaluation

Formal evaluation takes three main forms:

- Assessment of participants' immediate level of satisfaction with the course and the extent to which it achieved its objectives from their point of view.
- Measurement of the medium- or long-term impact of the training on individual participants' subsequent work performance.
- Measurement of the impact of the training on overall organizational performance and in relation to cost.

The use of end-of-course feedback from participants, with the aim of evaluating course design and delivery, has been described in Chapter 4.

Only if IST is evaluated is it possible to make informed improvements to course design, assess the extent to which objectives have been met, and judge whether further training is required and expenditure on IST is justifiable. However, because of the complexity of human behaviour and the vast array of factors which may affect it at any one time, evaluation of IST is not unproblematic; short of undertaking a major social research project, it is difficult to achieve 'scientific objectivity' in investigating the link between an IST programme and behavioural change. Similarly, the wide variety of factors which affect the quality (and *perceived* quality) of library service makes it difficult to isolate the organizational impact of IST. On the other hand, practical approaches to evaluating IST are available which take account of the complexity of organizational life, and which can do much to contribute to staff members' ongoing interpersonal skills development. Many of the general principles for evaluating training apply to evaluating IST; the points below highlight a few key and special considerations.[1]

6.2 Assessing changes in individual and group performance

- If the evaluation procedure enables the IST participant to reflect on and assess personal progress, the conditions for further learning will be created. Reviewing and evaluating achievement is a vital factor in experiential learning, and evaluation should be seen as a continuation of the learning process, stimulating further development.
- Analysis and evaluation of behaviour (whether one's own or that of someone else) is inevitably subjective and open to bias. Therefore evaluation of IST should always be carried out collaboratively, to combine self-assessment with feedback from appropriate colleagues. At least the IST participant and his or her manager should be involved in the process, and in many cases the training officer and perhaps other colleagues should participate.

- Evaluation criteria should relate closely to the training objectives (see Chapter 3), and therefore may be expressed in terms of behaviours, competences, attitudes, awareness, understanding or identify relevant communication structures and procedures. For instance, someone who has participated in training for running meetings effectively might be required to debrief her/his subsequent handling of a number of meetings with a line manager and to identify and evaluate her/his use of specified interpersonal skills in them. The outcomes of teamwork training on team members' attitudes and on the establishment of new work procedures likewise should be identifiable.
- Pre-course feedback and self-assessment is a useful preparation for participation in training and for post-course procedures (for instance, via briefings with managers).
- Participant feedback questionnaires or interviews administered 'downstream' of training are common and effective procedures, for instance, at three- to six-month intervals; comparison with immediate post-course responses may prove useful. Participants should be asked to provide concrete examples of how they judge the course has influenced performance at work. Colleague/line-management feedback can also be collected by questionnaire or face-to-face, based on clear observation criteria derived from the learning objectives of the IST course.
- Tests can be carried out to measure the cognitive aspect of participants' learning, for instance multiple-choice questions on telephone techniques.
- Keeping a journal is useful in the evaluation of personal learning, and it is possible to monitor progress both before and after the course in this way. An area such as time-management is especially amenable to the journal method of evaluation.
- Appraisal or performance review procedures provide ideal formats for combining line-management feedback with self-evaluation in relation to agreed performance objectives or competences. However, appraisal interviews are generally conducted only once or twice a year and need to cover a good deal of ground; the importance of follow-up debriefings to review the impact of individual IST events cannot be over-emphasized.

An example of a post-course IST evaluation questionnaire is given in Appendix 6.

6.3　Assessing organizational impact

Evaluation of the impact of IST on the general health of the library and its service means taking account of a combination of factors to gain a rounded picture, drawing on information and perspectives from IST participants, colleagues and clients. In cases where IST has been provided to solve a particular organizational or management problem or to establish new procedures, it should be possible to investigate whether the problem continues to exist, or the procedures are in place and functioning.

Depending on its objectives, evidence of the impact of IST on the organization might be found in the following:

- the findings of client satisfaction research, undertaken by means of questionnaires or interviews

- records of spontaneously expressed user satisfaction and of user complaints
- favourable attitudes to IST among staff
- the number and nature of requests made for training
- the availability of suitably skilled people to promote from within the organization
- the development of increasingly cooperative working relationships and structures
- enhanced staff morale and reduced absenteeism.

References

1   Phillips, S., *Evaluation*, London, Library Association, 1993.

 **IST planning checklist**

The check-list is intended as a brief, general outline of procedures and decisions involved in planning IST and is by no means exhaustive. It highlights major points made in the Guide.

7.1   **Respond to clearly identified training needs**

- Conduct regular, systematic IST needs analyses for the library as a whole and for occupational groups.
- Provide ongoing opportunities for assessing the IST needs of individual members of staff, preferably using their self-directed involvement in the process.
- Aim for a timely response to identified needs, at both organizational and individual levels.

7.2   **Consider policy and management issues**

- Is there a need for participation in any form of IST to be mandatory for all members of staff?
- Is adequate training in IST offered to in-house trainers and other appropriate staff to support the library's commitment to IST? Skills are needed in both the design and delivery of IST.

7.3   **Consider long-term development needs**

- What should the programme format be? A one-off event? An ongoing series of events?
- Is there a need for refresher programmes?
- How will on-the-job reinforcement be provided?

7.4   **Set learning aims and objectives**

- What should participants learn from the training? Be specific about objectives relating to knowledge, skills and attitudes and how learning will be demonstrated.
- What standard of performance should participants achieve as a result of training?

7.5   **Set process aims and objectives**

In general terms, how will participants learn? What type of training approach will be appropriate to meet the learning objectives?

- What are the likely learning preferences and anxieties of the training participants?

7.6 Plan overall design of training event

- Finalize the training group. What should the mix of participants be? What size of group?
- Determine available resources, including the number of trainers for the event; identify potential sources of training ideas and materials.
- Plan the structure of the training workshop. Identify a clear beginning, middle and end. Select activities for each part of the workshop.
- Plan the introductory session. How will introductions be handled? How will participants' learning objectives be identified? How much room for negotiation will there be within the programme? How will the ground-rules for group-work be set? How will 'housekeeping' details be covered?
- Select training methods and formats which will meet learning and process aims creatively and directly. Consider the wide range of possible methods and formats before making final decisions. Does the trainer have the necessary skills and confidence to facilitate the activities chosen?
- Plan the main sequence of learning activities according to the framework of the experiential learning cycle. Are experiential exercises followed by appropriate and adequate debriefing sessions and opportunities to plan or undertake further experimentation?
- Introduce concepts and skills in a logical order. Ensure that activities acknowledge and build on participants' prior experience.
- Does the choice and sequence of activities make sense in terms of managing the likely risk level in the group?
- Is there a reasonable variety of activities? Bear in mind constraints on resources such as space, number of trainers, size of group, etc.
- Build in opportunities for relaxation and fun.
- Build in opportunities for participants to evaluate their progress.
- Plan the workshop review session. Are participants given the opportunity to reflect on their own learning and consider follow-up actions? How will they provide evaluative feedback to the trainer? How is group closure achieved?
- Allocate a realistic time-scale for each activity, including breaks.

7.7 Plan each activity in detail and prepare materials

- Prepare handouts and resources to support learning activities.
- Prepare materials for trainer presentations (visual aids, etc.).
- Prepare personal notes for the trainer, outlining the workshop design and content.

7.8 Prepare post-training evaluation strategy

- How will the impact of the training on individual and group performance be assessed? Consider options according to available resources, and in the light of the need for a collaborative approach combining participants' self-assessment with feedback from colleagues.
- How will the impact of the training on the library's service or general organizational health be assessed? Aim to gain a rounded picture from a variety of indicators, both qualitative and quantitative, and evaluate findings in relation to costs incurred.

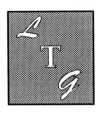

Appendix 1
Resources

Interpersonal skills and communication

Argyle, M., *Bodily communication*, (2nd edn), London, Methuen, 1988.

Argyle, M., *The psychology of interpersonal behaviour*, (4th edn), Harmondsworth, Penguin, 1983.

Argyle, M. (ed.), *Social skills and work*, London, Methuen, 1981.

Asanate, M. K. and Gudykunst, W. B., *Handbook of international and intercultural communications*, London, Sage, 1989.

Brislin, R. W. *et al.*, *Intercultural interactions: a practical guide*, London, Sage, 1986.

Caputo, J. S., *The assertive librarian*, New York, Oryx Press, 1984.

Cava, R., *Dealing with difficult people - proven strategies for handling stressful situations and defusing tensions*, London, Piatkus, 1990.

Egan, G., *The skilled helper: a systematic approach to effective helping*, (4th edn), Monterey, California, Brooks/Cole, 1990.

Hargie, O. (ed.), *A handbook of communication skills*, London, Croom Helm, 1986,

Hargie, O. *et al.*, *Social skills in interpersonal communication*, (2nd edn), London, Croom Helm, 1987.

Mathews, A. J., *Communicate! A librarian's guide to interpersonal relations*, Chicago, American Library Association, 1983.

Nelson-Jones, R., *Human relationship skills: training and self-help*, London, Cassell, 1986.

Nelson-Jones, R., *Practical counselling and helping skills*, (2nd edn), London, Cassell, 1988.

Interpersonal skills training and development

Barker, D. M., *TA and training: the theory and use of transactional analysis in organizations*, Aldershot, Gower, 1980.

Clark, N., *Managing personal learning and change: a trainer's guide*, London, McGraw-Hill, 1991.

Clarke, D. and Underwood, J., *Assertion training*, Cambridge, National Extension College, 1988.

Cooper, S. and Heenan, C., *Preparing, designing and leading workshops: a humanistic approach*, London, Van Nostrand Reinhold, 1980.

Cronin, B. and Martin, I., 'Social skills training in librarianship', *Journal of librarianship*, **15** (2) 1983, 105–22.

Dainow, S. and Bailey, C., *Developing skills with people: training for person to person client contact*, Chichester, Wiley, 1988.

Forbess-Greene, S., *The encyclopedia of ice-breakers: structured activities that warm-up, motivate, challenge, acquaint and energize*, San Diego, California, University Associates, 1983.

Heron, J., *The facilitator's handbook*, London, Kogan Page, 1989.

Hollin, C. R. and Trower, P., *Handbook of social skills training (Vols 1 and 2)*, Oxford, Pergamon, 1986.

Inskipp, F., *A manual for trainers: resource book for setting up and running basic counselling courses*, London, Alexia, 1985.

Kelley, C., *Assertion training: a facilitator's guide*, San Diego, California, University Associates, 1979.

Lago, C., *Working with overseas students: a staff development training manual*, London, British Council/Polytechnic of Huddersfield, 1991.

Levy, P. and Usherwood, B., *People skills: interpersonal skills training for library and information work*, (Library and Information Research Report 88), London, British Library, 1992.

Nelson-Jones, R., *Lifeskills, a handbook*, London, Cassell, 1991.

Pfeiffer, J. W., *Reference guide to handbooks and manuals*, San Diego, California, University Associates, 1985.

Pfeiffer, J. W. and Ballew, A. C., *Design skills in human resource development*, San Diego, California, University Associates, 1988.

Pfeiffer, J. W. and Ballew, A. C., *Presentation and evaluation skills in human resource development*, San Diego, California, University Associates, 1988.

Pfeiffer, J. W., Jones, J. E. and Goodstein, L. D. (eds.), The *Annual* series for human resource practitioners, San Diego, California, University Associates, 1972–.

Phillips, K. and Fraser, T., *The management of interpersonal skills training*, Aldershot, Gower, 1982.

Pont, T., *Developing effective training skills*, London, McGraw-Hill, 1991.

Prytherch, R. (ed.), *Handbook of library training practice*, Aldershot, Gower, 1986

Rae, L., *The skills of human relations training*, Aldershot, Gower, 1985.

Ross, C. and Dewdney, P., *Communicating professionally: a how-to-do-it manual for librarians*, New York, Neal-Schuman, 1990.

Taylor, D. S. and Wright, P. L., *Developing interpersonal skills through tutored practice*, London, Prentice Hall, 1988.

Thorne, M. L. and Fritchie, R., *Interpersonal skills for women managers: a tutor's guide*, Bristol Polytechnic/Manpower Services Commission, 1985.

Learning methods

Adair, J. *et al.*, *A handbook of management training exercises*, (Vols 1 and 2), London, British Association of Commercial and Industrial Education, 1980–2.

Bond, T., *Games for social and life skills*, London, Hutchinson, 1986.

Brandes, D., *Gamesters 2*, London, Hutchinson, 1982.

Brandes, D. and Phillips, H., *Gamesters' handbook: 140 games for teachers and group leaders*, London, Hutchinson, 1977.

Jones, K., *A sourcebook of management simulations*, London, Kogan Page, 1989.

Jones, N., 'Learning in groups: strategies for group-work in education and training for library management', *Education for information*, **4** (1), 1986, 27–45

Jones, N. and Jordan, P., *Case studies in library management*, London, Bingley, 1988.

Pfeiffer, J. W. and Ballew, A. C., *Using case studies, simulations and games in human resource development*, San Diego, California, University Associates, 1988.

Pfeiffer, J. W. and Ballew, A. C., *Using instruments in human resource development*, San Diego, California, University Associates, 1988.

Pfeiffer, J. W. and Ballew, A. C., *Using lecturettes, theory and models in human resource development*, San Diego, California, University Associates, 1988.

Pfeiffer, J. W. and Ballew, A. C., *Using role plays in human resource development*, San Diego, California, University Associates, 1988.

Pfeiffer, J. W. and Ballew, A. C., *Using structured experiences in human resource development*, San Diego, California, University Associates, 1988.

Pfeiffer, J. W. and Jones, J. E. (eds.), *A handbook of structured experiences for human relations training (Vols.1-10)*, San Diego, California, University Associates, 1969, 1970, 1971, 1973, 1975, 1977, 1979, 1981, 1983, 1985.

Van Ments, M., *The effective use of role-play*, (2nd edn), London, Kogan Page, 1989.

Weeks, H. W. *et al. A manual of structured experiences for cross-cultural learning*, Yarmouth, Maine, Intercultural Press, 1977.

Videos

Assertiveness: effective interaction with library users, available from: Dept. of Library and Information Studies, Manchester Metropolitan University, All Saints, Manchester M15 6BH. Tel. 061-247 2000. Illustrates assertiveness techniques and concepts through role-play.

Awkward colleagues, available from: Media Services, Learning Resources, University of Brighton, Watts Building, Moulsecoomb, Brighton BN2 4GJ. Tel. 0273 600900. Trigger video made up of 26 'behind-the-scenes' problems between staff.

Awkward libraries, available from University of Brighton, as above. Trigger video showing inappropriate staff responses to readers' enquiries.

Awkward readers, available from University of Brighton, as above. Trigger video depicting problems encountered at a library issue or enquiry desk.

Communication skills in libraries; Aggression in libraries; Overseas students in libraries; in first instance, contact Stephen Cox, School of Art and Design, Coventry University, Priory Street, Coventry CV1 5FB. Tel. 0203 631313.

Hear and now, available from: United Kingdom Council for Overseas Students' Affairs, 9–17 St. Albans Place, Islington, London N1 0NX. Tel. 071-226 3762. Overseas students presenting their personal, academic and financial difficulties.

Multi-racial videoscenes, available from: Dept of Educational Technology, De Montfort University, PO Box 143, Leicester. Tel. 0533 551551. Trigger video on theme of helping people from different cultural and racial backgrounds.

Survey of training materials, May 1988, issued by the Education Department, The Library Association, 7 Ridgmount Street, London WC1 7AE. Tel. 071-636 7543. Contains references to a wide variety of interpersonal skills training videos and other types of audiovisual training materials used in libraries. No update available at time of writing.

Resource organizations

BBC Training Videos, BBC Enterprises Ltd., Woodlands, 80 Wood Lane, London W12 0TT.

Concorde Video and Film Council, 201 Felixstowe Road, Ipswich IP3 9BJ. Tel. 0743 715754. Wide range of materials on topics such as working with groups, counselling techniques, race, gender and cross-cultural issues, violence.

Local Government Management Board, Arndale House, Arndale Centre, Luton, Bedfordshire LU1 2TS. Tel. 0582 451166. Materials on all aspects of training and IST for the public sector.

Video Arts Ltd, 68 Oxford Street, London W1. Tel. 071-637 7288. Video and other materials on a wide range of interpersonal skills topics, mainly explored within private-sector organizational settings.

Appendix 2
Personal Learning Review Questionnaire

This questionnaire is for you to record your immediate reactions to the workshop. It is for your own future reference and does not need to be handed back to the trainer.

1. What I have learned about interpersonal skills...

2. What I have learned about interpersonal skills training...

3. What I have learned about myself...

4. What I have learned about working in this group...

5. What I have done well...

6. What I have found difficult...

7. What I aim to do differently as a result of the workshop...

Appendix 3
IST Course Evaluation Form

Please fill this in and hand it back to the trainer before leaving. Circle the rating you feel is most appropriate in each case, and add any further comments. For the rating scale, (1) is the most positive response and (5) the most negative.

1. What did you hope to gain from the course?

2. To what extent do you feel it helped you to achieve your aims? How?

    to a very great extent 1 2 3 4 5 not at all

3. To what extent do you think what you have done on the course will be helpful in your work? How?

    to a very great extent 1 2 3 4 5 not at all

4. What aspects of the course did you find most helpful?

5. What aspects of the course did you find least helpful?

6. How could the course have usefully been different?

7. Any other comments?

Appendix 4
Library staffing matters: case studies

You are the Librarian of a multi-site University. The problems below are reported to you. Indicate the short-term and long-term action you would take, and what you would say to the member(s) of staff involved.

1   One of the library assistants, Sandra, is consistently late for work. The Senior Library Assistant has spoken to her about this before, but to no effect. The SLA is puzzled by the problem, since the reference from her previous employer, the British Library, made no mention of this, and she was keen to move to the area with her fiancé – they have recently married.

2.   A young professional, Brian, has recently been interviewed for a more senior post within the small site library where he works. An external candidate was appointed. The site librarian has been dissatisfied with his work for some time, but Brian is bitterly disappointed and this is obvious to other staff.

3.   A lecturer has complained that a member of the library staff refused to let him borrow books which he needed for a seminar. He has written a strongly worded memorandum, in which he accuses the staff of being rude and obstreperous about petty rules.

4.   Shirley, a Section Head, is suffering from overwork. She often works late, yet she constantly misses deadlines for important tasks, including a financial report to the Librarian.

(Cases used in Assistant Librarian Professional Training
Programme on Managing Staff, Sheffield Hallam University
Library; devised by Karen Stanton)

Appendix 5
Example role-play:
Giving feedback

The role-play is conducted in groups of four. One person takes on the 'giving feedback' role and another the 'receiving feedback' role. The others act as observers.

Confidential briefing: 'Giving feedback'

In the usual run of things, you get on well with your boss, Head of Community Services, and admire his/her ability to respond quickly to situations and to think well 'on the wing'.

However, your boss often has difficulty organizing his/her workload and meeting deadlines. This means you become involved in last-minute panics when s/he asks you to drop everything and help with the task in hand.

For instance, yesterday morning s/he was preparing to talk to a group of youth workers. The talk had been planned for some time, but s/he had kept putting off the preparation. You had to rearrange your own schedule on the enquiry desk and postpone a meeting in order to help gather up materials and help plan the talk.

You have decided, the following morning, to explain your point of view and challenge your boss on this issue. You ask to have a word. Your aim is to use your feedback skills to make your point and then to go on to agree a different way of working together for the future.

Confidential briefing: 'Receiving feedback'

You are Head of Community Services for a public library service. Yesterday, you carried out a successful talk to a group of youth workers. A member of your team helped you to prepare the overhead slides and other materials and plan the talk in the morning prior to the talk.

This colleague has asked to have a word with you. You are very busy and do not know what s/he wants to talk about. Your mind is on a meeting you have to attend later in the day, and you feel a little irritated at the interruption to your preparations for it.

However, you agree to see him/her as you are sure it can't be a lengthy matter.

Appendix 6
Post-Course Evaluation Questionnaire

Teamwork Skills Course

1. To what extent do you agree with the following statements?

(a) Generally, my team is working better as a result of the course.

[ ] strongly agree
[ ] agree
[ ] neutral
[ ] disagree
[ ] strongly disagree

Please briefly explain your answer.

(b) I am working better as a team member as a result of the course.

[ ] strongly agree
[ ] agree
[ ] neutral
[ ] disagree
[ ] strongly disagree

Please briefly explain your answer.

2. To what extent did the course fulfil the following aims?

(a) To provide an opportunity for colleagues to share experiences, ideas, views

fully 1 2 3 4 5 not at all

(b) To identify skills for productive teamwork

fully 1 2 3 4 5 not at all

(c) To relate the skills to situations experienced by team members

fully 1 2 3 4 5 not at all

3. Please list up to five 'productive ways forward' for your team identified during the workshop:

4. Which, if any, have been put into practice since?

5. How would you rate the overall value of the course?

(a) To yourself

   very valuable 1 2 3 4 5 no value

(b) To your team

   very valuable 1 2 3 4 5 no value

6. What follow-up has there been to the course?

7. What, if any, further follow-up do you think there should be?

   (a) for you personally?

   (b) for your team?

8. Any further comments?

Thank you.

(Example adapted from a questionnaire designed by Susan Dudley for a training course at the Library of the University of the West of England, Bristol)

Figure 1
Core skills for library and
information work

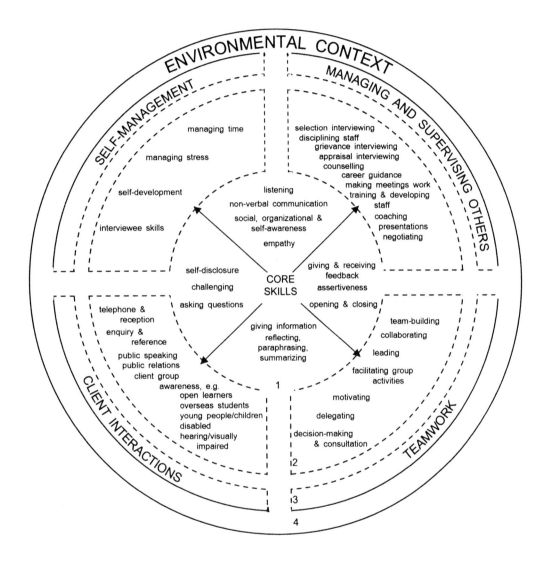

Zone 1   Core skills
Zone 2   Applications
Zone 3   Skills in library and information context
Zone 4   Environmental context

Figure 2
Kolb's Experiential Learning Cycle

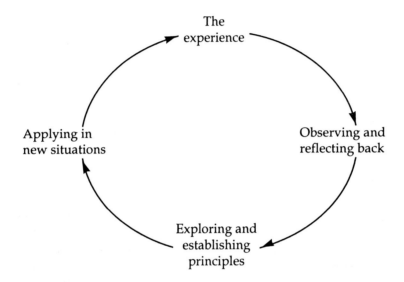

Index